TASMAN
TRESPASSER II

TASMAN
TRESPASSER II

The Shaun Quincey Story

SHAUN QUINCEY

HarperCollins*Publishers*

HarperCollins*Publishers*

First published in 2010
by HarperCollins*Publishers* (New Zealand) Limited
PO Box 1, Shortland Street, Auckland 1140

HarperCollins*Publishers*
31 View Road, Glenfield, Auckland 0627, New Zealand
25 Ryde Road, Pymble, Sydney, NSW 2073, Australia
A 53, Sector 57, Noida, UP, India
77–85 Fulham Palace Road, London W6 8JB, United Kingdom
2 Bloor Street East, 20th floor, Toronto, Ontario M4W 1A8, Canada
10 East 53rd Street, New York, NY 10022, USA

National Library of New Zealand Cataloguing-in-Publication Data

Quincey, Shaun.
Tasman Trespasser II : the Shaun Quincey story / Shaun Quincey.
ISBN 978-1-86950-891-3
1. Quincey, Shaun. 2. Tasman Trespasser II (Boat)
3. Rowing—Tasman Sea.
I. Title.
910.916478—dc 22

Cover design by Carolyn Lewis
Cover images courtesy *New Zealand Geographic* (front) and *New Zealand Herald* (back)
Typesetting by Springfield West

Printed by Griffin Press, Australia

70gsm Classic used by HarperCollins*Publishers* is a natural, recyclable product made from wood grown in sustainable forests. The manufacturing processes conform to the environmental regulations in the country of origin, Finland.

To Lisa Jones, Michael Buck, Winton Jones, Jill Jones, Oliver Young, Colin Quincey and Nitaya Quincey — I will never forget Team Tasman and the effort you all put in at the last minute to get me and TTII *ready for our big adventure.*

Thank you.

TO THE PEOPLE OF NZ

*Somebody said that it couldn't be done
But he with a chuckle replied,
That 'Maybe it couldn't but he would be one
Who wouldn't say so — till he'd tried.'*

*There are thousands to tell you it cannot be done
There are thousands to prophesy failure
There are thousands to point to you one by one
The dangers that will assail you.*

*But just buckle in with a grin
Then take off your coat and go to it
Just start in to sing as you tackle the thing
That 'cannot be done' and you'll do it.*

A poem written by a schoolgirl to my father, Colin Quincey.

Contents

Appendices

Where it all began

It's November 2008 and I'm bored. I'm swimming 2.8 km in the Auckland Harbour Crossing, rather hung over after a slightly indulgent surfboat carnival the previous day. As I finish the race I realize I've been looking for something. Something to absorb my life, something to take over my thoughts and drive me to a new head space, where limits, rules and critics no longer exist and ultimate freedom is tasted and survived.

Like a lot of people, every day I dream up a new idea or a better way of doing things, and now I think that my trip across the Tasman was one of those dreams I just decided put into action. It didn't come from nowhere, though — in 1977 my father, Colin Quincey, rowed his boat, *Tasman Trespasser*, from Hokianga Harbour, in the North Island of New Zealand, to Marcus Beach, on Australia's Gold Coast. He crossed the Tasman Sea in 63 days and seven hours, becoming the first person to do it solo.

Whether it was something in Auckland Harbour that day or the bump on the head from the surfboat the day before, it dawned on me that I couldn't settle any longer for the nine-to-five routine. There has to be more, I tell myself, as I climb up the finishing ramp, slightly confused and depressed. Not the usual response after completing a race I reflected, and came to the conclusion that dramatic change was needed.

Why the Tasman? I still don't know the complete answer. I simply woke up and decided I would give it a crack. I firmly believe a combination of events determines whether your goal will come to fruition, and I was lucky enough and driven enough to make sure critical factors and events fell into place. I can certainly identify some key driving factors. My father's trip has always made me wonder whether I could accomplish something similar, and at the time I'd had more than enough doom and gloom about recession and tough times. I decided to take it upon myself to prove that New Zealand is still exciting and a breeding ground for adventure and success. Strangely enough, a sick and twisted part of me thought it would be fun.

As a result of my decision, I've never been more scared, had less money, been laughed at so much, nor been as unprepared for what I was about to attempt. Throughout the whole journey I never knew what was going to happen next, or if I even had the ability to pull it together.

Transforming an idea into reality is life-changing. At that stage I had no idea that *Tasman Trespasser II* was an idea that would take 18 months of my life and dominate it completely. Throughout that time I held a vision of arriving on the shores of New Zealand and how the powerful feeling of that arrival would ultimately dissolve memories of hard times in the campaign and terrifying moments in the Tasman. When it finally did happen, the memory and emotion of that arrival was huge, something I will carry for the rest of my life. It's way more important than any sum of money or amount of property. Someone once said to me: 'If who you are is what you've got and what you've got is lost, then who are you?', which constantly reminds me that you are defined and remembered by your actions, not your salary. It was a huge motivating force for me.

Why is such a hard question to answer, especially when *why not* is so much easier. I suppose I've consistently challenged the status quo my entire life, and, to be honest, set the odd unrealistic goal for myself. I don't know why, but I get more gratification searching for the single reason why we *should* try something rather than settling for the 1001 reasons why we shouldn't.

Rowing the Tasman was something I knew I could achieve, but I also knew it would push me to my limits. I had found a test I was ready to attack.

With an email to Salthouse Boatbuilders the chain to the nine-to-five routine was cut and the *Tasman Trespasser II* campaign was born.

1 Twenty-six houses

Dark engulfing clouds surrounded the boat most of today, with splatters of lightning decorating the sky. Every so often I wonder if sooner or later one will hit the boat. All the aerials on the boat are humming, and I wonder if perhaps it's the static electricity in the air. Who knows? Terrified at the thought of a lightning strike, I put on my lifejacket and attach the safety harness. With water crashing against the cabin door every so often, I know I'll only have a few seconds to get out the door and clip on before the next wave engulfs me and *TTII*.

In the lull of a wave I snap open the cabin door at precisely the wrong moment. I'm hit by a wave and pushed halfway back into the cabin, along with five or so litres of water. With no time for thought I launch headfirst out the cabin door, reaching around behind me to slam it shut to avoid more water getting into the cabin. Wearing nothing but a lifejacket clipped onto a steel wire in an effort to preserve some dry clothing, I stand up to peer over the back of the boat.

I can see nothing but crashing waves, every single one with the potential to capsize us. I constantly try to be positive and grateful for being out here, but today is not one of those days. It is 7 p.m. and I have lost around 75 km of distance. I am wet, cold and hungry and wonder what on earth has led me to this point.

I was born on 27 September 1984, in Singapore. Dad, who was English, was in the Royal New Zealand Navy at the time, serving in some remote little town. My older brother Ben was three when I was born, and I assume we all lived quite happily together, having no real memories of my own from that time. My family spent a few years in Singapore and Malaysia before eventually moving back to New Zealand, and straight to Devonport.

Now a fairly well-established and affluent suburb, at the time it was more of an up-and-coming working-class area and home of the New Zealand Navy. Devonport was a great little village to grow up in; we had a tidy Navy house just above a small and basically private beach where my brother and I would spend a lot of time adventuring. I remember building massive, elaborate tree houses in the old pohutukawa trees, and trying to build the next-best hut in the root systems of dangling trees on the cliff at Narrow Neck Beach.

The family only lasted a few years at 11 Gillespie Place before Mum and Dad went their separate ways and my brother and I were introduced to words like lawyers, full custody and guidance counselling. A long and drawn-out divorce resulted in me living with Mum and Ben living with Dad. Every second weekend I would catch up with Ben and in hindsight I'm gutted I didn't grow up side by side with my brother. Sadly, I think we were both slightly tainted with the brush of each parent's perspective on the other parent, which sometimes made our relationship a struggle.

On the positive side, though, I believe the situation allowed me to develop a sense of independence from very early on, which probably stemmed from being asked, as a seven year old, who I wanted to live with. I also learned to develop people skills, such as meeting my parents' new partners and their kids. I had to quickly adapt to sharing holidays and events with new people, after basically being told I had to like them. As a result I learned very early on to manage relationships in a variety of situations.

I went to Vauxhall Primary, a wonderful school where I was lucky enough to make some great friends, and I still share beers with them today. After Vauxhall I went on to Belmont Intermediate, which wasn't so great.

It was a strange time for me as Dad was moving down to live in Christchurch, leaving me in Auckland with Mum. I'd really been looking forward to going on to the same high school as my brother, but he was moving to Christchurch with Dad. Even though I was only 12, I knew having a dad around was important, but for the next seven years I would only catch up with mine maybe two or three times a year.

I got the feeling his partner at the time didn't want me around the house. To be fair I didn't care much for her either, after she left the gate open and our family dog of 13 years was run over. Dad's relationship with this particular woman deteriorated somewhat after the dog incident and he ended up moving out to a beach house near Brighton. It was bloody terrific to get free time with the old man again!

I spent my high school years at Takapuna Grammar on Auckland's North Shore, a fantastic school where I was able to get stuck into every possible opportunity and would eventually become Head Boy. Takapuna Grammar was also the first opportunity I had to try out rowing. I was 14 and at the time

TGS had some fairly high-performing rowers in the sixth and seventh forms, including Hamish Allison and Grey Gilbert, a couple of great role models to aspire to and try to beat. I remember my first erg (rowing machine — short for ergometer) training session where we had to row 2000 m as fast as we could. This was horrific and by far one of the most painful exercises I'd ever done.

I'd played rugby my entire life as a prop and this eight-minute work-out compared to nothing I'd ever done before; after tears, vomit and a quick trip to the toilet, I reflected on the satisfaction of completing my first 2 km on a rower. This was also my first opportunity to reflect on my father's achievements.

I sat on that machine in awe, wondering how on earth that skinny old bugger rowed 2200 km when I was 90 per cent dead after rowing 2 km. And he smoked!

High school was a big intersection where I was presented with so many possible paths to follow. Dad was an advocate for freedom and letting me do what I wanted, whether it was leaving school to travel or playing whatever sport. As long as I was paying my way and not being lazy, Dad was happy. Dad always thought I was fat, cheekily claiming I had my mother's genes, and I have to say he was fairly accurate about me being chubby. I would spin it around and tell him that if I lost weight then he would have to give up smoking, which would soon end the conversation and we'd end up talking about rugby or something else.

I spent 95 per cent of my time with Mum and my first step-father, an ex-army officer who had served in the Vietnam War. Throughout my high school years he issued me with strict rules — a three-minute time limit in the shower, room inspections before school, complete silence around the house and enforced table etiquette. I battled with the routine, which at times was rigidly enforced and at other times relaxed, but it stood me in good stead for years to come, when it helped to have a few rules and the ability to draw on some old routines and disciplines.

Trouble started to brew when I was between the ages of 14 and 17 and the effects of the Vietnam War came to fruition for my stepdad. The Major had little control of his temper and this, combined with what would eventually be diagnosed as bipolar disorder with post-traumatic stress disorder and, I strongly suspect, some 'Agent Orange' illnesses, led to the demise of the relatively successful business he ran with Mum. In the process our family was declared bankrupt when I was 18, on the eve of my Bursary English exam. Mum was left to deal with a lot of this in what was a very testing time for the family, and full credit to Mum. Stripped of her financial assets and sticking by a disturbed husband, she managed somehow to hold it all together for a long time, before she would eventually end the marriage and have to start again.

I credit that time in my life with developing some helpful skills which I believe got me through some of the harder times. At one stage I remember adding up how many houses I had lived in by the time I was 17 and it was 26.

I felt a level of responsibility for my mother's well-being and happiness and I certainly battled with what my stepfather's illness and his volatile temper and stubbornness had done. I know I was very frustrated, not knowing how to help.

Fortunately for me, I had a couple of great homes-away-from-home during that period of my life. My then-girlfriend Caroline Collard and her family were fantastic, and we went on some great trips away together. They always opened the door if I needed somewhere to go and study or to just relax away from home. I was also into lifesaving by then and had the surf-lifesaving club as another refuge. With rugby as well, the only reason to go home was to sleep and eat. My weekends in winter were filled with rugby and the weekends in summer were filled with surfboat racing and surf-lifesaving.

I had my University Entrance and managed to scrape through Bursary, so with no real idea of what I wanted to do I enrolled at Auckland University for a Bachelor of Commerce. I managed to stay there for the first semester before being offered an internship at Surf Lifesaving New Zealand, down in Wellington.

One of my old PE teachers from Takapuna Grammar, Brett Sullivan, had a job there and I became one of his assistants, managing the freight and storage systems and running the senior lifeguard training schools. I stayed there for a couple of years, taking advantage of the opportunity to complete a few economics papers at Victoria University.

Mum had ended the relationship with my first stepfather when I was 18 and found some work on a farm in the Marlborough Sounds, which was great because work wasn't the only thing she found down there. When I was living in Wellington I was struck down with a virus and Mum decided she would come and visit me with her new partner, whom I hadn't met yet. I was slightly excited and also a little nervous because of how her last relationship ended, and I was hoping this guy was a kind and down-to-earth sort of bloke I would get along with.

Graham Stewart was his name and he came across as very quiet and also very nervous about meeting me. As Mum told me later, he was terrified I might not like him. One of the kindest and most gentle men I have ever met, he was an ex-merchant seaman and treated my mum with an incredible amount of

17

love and respect, which in my eyes gave him a massive tick in the box. Graham eventually asked Mum to get married but tragically a few weeks after the wedding he was diagnosed with cancer, which had spread through a large proportion of his body.

A kinder man couldn't have died a worse death. Over the next two years the cancer slowly worked its way through his body and he spent his final year incapacitated, moving between hospice, hospital and home, with Mum nursing him. Over the time Graham was dying I had some of the most wonderful and insightful conversations with him about absolutely everything he had done in his life in the Merchant Navy, and his children.

I would sometimes cry listening to his stories and other times fall off my chair laughing. I slowly grew very close to this wonderful man and watching him die slowly with painful cancer just didn't seem right, especially after all the love and kindness he had shown my family. Graham eventually died on 25 June 2008, incredibly sad but also a relief for everyone, as there would be no more trips to the hospice or hospital to watch him in pain. It was the end of another rollercoaster journey for my family and a tough road for Mum. Graham's death certainly got me thinking about what direction I wanted to take my life in and provided me with some massive insights as to what was important.

As Surf started to become too much like work I began to miss racing surfboats and weekends away with mates at surf competitions. Eventually, I resigned and moved back to Auckland, where I enrolled as a full-time student at the

Auckland University of Technology. To make ends meet I worked as well, running a call centre, and with racing surfboats and study, this routine filled the next couple of years.

By now I was 22, flatting in Auckland and chipping away at uni quite happily. I completed 90 per cent of my degree and decided I wanted to work full time while I studied part time, as I was fairly sick of the student lifestyle and not having any money.

I applied as a radio advertising salesperson and got the job with no idea of what I was really in for. At the call centre I had been hand-managing 30 telemarketers working from 3 p.m. till 9 p.m. each night but had never really ventured out on the street to sell anything, let alone radio advertising.

In a massive challenge I was sent to an area which didn't receive radio reception, and as the market was generally local businesses this was tricky, to say the least. It all proved rather fruitless, even after helping to install radio aerials on a number of businesses to convince them that what I was selling did exist.

I began to develop a small business on the side selling advertising on takeaway coffee cups to supplement my income. As the coffee-cup concept gathered some momentum I decided my time was better spent working on the cups and I left my team of radio mates to go and work on my idea. I created a small company and distribution network around Auckland before being approached by an Australian company looking to set up in New Zealand. After a few frustrating challenges printing the cups I was offered a reasonable amount of money for my business plan and the relationships I had made and I decided to take the offer and move on.

Slightly lost as to what I would do next, I found myself applying as an account manager in an Occupational Therapy provider looking to break into the corporate world. After just one month I knew I had made a mistake, but I needed the work experience to complete certain elements of my university degree and by now I was relying on the income and company car. This was when it occurred to me that I certainly did not want to spend the rest of my life doing something like this, and that I needed to break the mould in some way or another. The Tasman concept started to slowly brew.

2 Quincey developing

At a very early age I was introduced to sport, playing soccer from when I was about five. It didn't take long for Mum and Dad to realize I wasn't best suited to the game as I started tackling most of the other kids and would always end up in the goal. I happily moved to the rugby field at around seven, with memories of playing on frosted fields in bare feet that typically haunt a lot of young Kiwi rugby players. Rugby was to dominate most of my sporting life from that point onwards. I absolutely loved the game, slowly progressing through different age groups and teams as I grew up with a collection of great mates.

The only problem with rugby was that Mum hated the game and every single year there would be a week-long battle, which always involved tears from Mum as I would go about convincing her it was a great game and I would be playing no matter what.

I never stopped playing rugby and when I was 11 I was introduced to its swimming equivalent, the probably more vicious game of water polo. I loved swimming and water polo was a challenging, aggressive team sport. More importantly, the two sports didn't clash. Water polo and rugby dominated my high school years and I started to focus more on rugby after trialling for the first XV in the third form and eventually getting my first games for the top school team in the fourth form.

I loved the spirit of playing in the top school team and was lucky enough to have a couple of very good coaches as role models to steer me in the right direction while I was at school, keeping me fit and in line when the need arose.

Towards the end of my fourth form year I was selected in a rugby development squad to travel to Japan and play a number of games. This trip would be one of my schooling highlights as we travelled around Japan for three weeks. We were billeted out to different Japanese families and played rugby constantly. It was an absolute adventure and made a huge difference to the level of rugby being played at Takapuna Grammar.

A few years later the school decided to travel to the Gold Coast of Australia for another rugby tour, the first time I had been to Australia. It was another great trip and because we were a bit older there were a few more fun adventures off the field. One day driving north a sign to Marcus Beach caught my eye. Dad's expedition across the Tasman didn't really get talked about that much, but I did remember he had landed at Marcus Beach, and as our bus passed the sign I wondered if one day I'd get the chance to come back and explore the beach.

I was hindered with a couple of serious knee injuries when I was 16, tearing the cartilage in my knee and requiring surgery. Much to Mum's relief this took me out of rugby for a year, which I spent coaching an under-16 side.

Rowing had only really entered the picture when I was 14 and it was out of curiosity that I decided I'd give it a try and jumped in the school rowing eight with a few of my rugby mates. I'd been in a rowing skiff once before and I was thrown in with the senior eight crew for an endurance race down the Waikato River, very nervously because of my lack of experience.

After a rough start my technique improved and we happily rowed down the river. As we approached a number of girls' crews temptation got the better of me and I burst out in song with the other guys eventually repeating my poetic words, using lyrics a few years beyond my time. Unfortunately, one of the girls' parents heard me and I was pointed out as the singing ring leader. I was called into an office the next week to be told that I was now on the ultra-strict rowing warning system, which was basically one warning and then you're out on your ear, which, combined with an annual rowing fee of $2000, was enough for me to decide to move on from school rowing very quickly.

With winters spent happily playing rugby and the odd bit of water polo when rugby allowed some time off, I started to crave a summer sport that would keep me extra busy and away from home. I was sitting in a school classroom when my friend started telling me he'd like to work as a surf lifeguard and become a surf ironman. I absolutely loved the sound of it and began to investigate how to get started as soon as I got home. We checked out a few surf clubs and asked some of the teachers we knew were involved. The closest one was Mairangi Bay, so we decided to take a look.

Within weeks we were enrolled to become surf lifesavers. I fell in love with surf lifesaving and the culture of spending most of my time on the beach, either training or just surfing in the waves. This would also be my first introduction to being put in a serious position of responsibility as a surf lifeguard. When I qualified I was told I could possibly become a paid lifeguard if I obtained a few more qualifications, trained hard and improved my confidence in the surf. Excited by the prospect of saving a

23

life combined with spending all day on the beach and getting paid for it, I made it my mission to be working as a lifeguard by the next summer. I spent the winter months completing courses in first aid and risk management programmes as I prepared for the summer ahead. As paid lifeguard positions were highly contested, I needed to trial against a number of other candidates, completing a written test as well as a 400 m swim and 5 km run.

A few days after the trial I was accepted and told I'd be working as a paid lifeguard over summer. I was nervous and excited about venturing into dangerous surf to rescue someone from drowning, knowing that if I didn't do my job well lives would be at risk. Thankfully, my first few weeks were on very calm east coast beaches and I spent most of the time treating bee stings and helping people with directions. My third week of work I was posted to the fairly intense west coast beach Karekare where over the years there have been a number of deaths as a result of the massive surf and currents.

There were three of us in the team and as the beach wasn't that busy we rotated the watch position on the tower, completing half an hour each. By 1 p.m. I had completed three watches when out of the corner of my eye I saw what I thought looked like a hand in the air — a distress signal. Grabbing the binoculars I saw a female swimmer just about to get dumped by a fairly big wave. I radioed my team, telling them I needed help, and was mentally heading into the water before I'd even grabbed my tube and jumped off the tower. I took the quad motorbike down the beach, slightly panicked as to what I should do next. I waved to my team, who were running down the beach, and ran into the water with tube in tow and flippers in my hand.

24

The swimmer was only about 100 m out, but she was stuck in a big deep hole and being constantly dumped on by the surf. The fear in her eyes was intense as she screamed for help, and I was out to her in a few moments. Sliding the rescue tube across the water for her to hold, I swam around behind her to clip her in and start swimming to shore. Unwilling or unable by then to kick, she was certainly a dead weight and my team ran out to help me swim her into the beach. The adrenaline was completely pumping and I couldn't believe how great it felt to pull someone out of the water.

She was very grateful and came back to the beach a few hours later with a donation for the club. After my first rescue I was completely hooked and knew I would be a surf lifeguard for the rest of my life. The feeling of successfully pulling someone out of the water alive was fantastic and it was incredibly gratifying being able to provide a much needed service when people were in trouble.

I continued to worked as a surf lifeguard throughout summer, which kept me in fairly good condition for the coming rugby season. I absolutely loved the surf and couldn't think of anything better to be doing.

That feeling didn't last long. Within a few months I was told I might never play rugby or work as a surf lifeguard again.

3 Quincey + bath of soapy water = washing machine

At 17 years of age I was deemed responsible enough to spend a few nights in a family friend's house looking after Jamie, their 13-year-old boy. A relatively simple task, which was running fairly smoothly. It was a Saturday night and after playing rugby I'd headed down to my friend's 21st party for a few beers before arriving at the house in time to see the family head away for a break. Jamie and I and my girlfriend at the time watched a movie and it was a fairly quiet night, with everyone in bed before midnight.

I woke up at around 7 a.m. feeling completely normal but started twitching a bit here and there. Getting out of bed and walking were a challenge, though funnily enough, this seemed normal to me. Over the past few years I had woken up with similar symptoms and had been known to smash glasses in the kitchen trying to fill the glass with water or suddenly fall over. I took these symptoms in my stride and put them down to early morning twitches and had convinced myself they were a standard event and not to be fussed about. I actually thought they were rather funny. I caught myself weeing up a wall at one stage and had also accidentally thrown a number of drinks at people. I'd always put it down to normal little twitches that I thought everyone got from time to time. What I didn't know was that I was epileptic.

That Sunday morning I stumbled up the stairs at around 7.30 and collapsed onto Jamie's stereo and launched into a five- or six-minute tonic-clonic epileptic seizure. Later Jamie told me he initially thought I was playing a joke on him, spitting, moaning and groaning. This idea slowly diminished as my face went purple and blood started pouring out of my mouth — by then I'd bitten down on my tongue.

My girlfriend came up the stairs to find me like this and thankfully called the ambulance. I was still unconscious when they arrived and would be incoherent for close to two hours.

I had suffered a massive seizure and could not recall anything about it — all I remember is waking up in hospital and the doctor asking me if I had taken any drugs the night before. I was absolutely exhausted and had never felt so physically tired. Whether it was the rugby game the day before or just the effect of the seizure, I was stuffed and slept for the rest of the day.

The tiredness was gone within a few days but what was plaguing my mind was what it all meant. I was banned from driving on my discharge papers and told I couldn't play sport until I had seen a neurologist, and promptly put onto a seven-month waiting list. I couldn't wait that long to get back to rowing surfboats and playing rugby, so Mum and I went to see a private neurologist. There I was plugged into a few machines and went through a series of tests, including being told to breathe in and out as fast as I could, lights were flashed in front of me and then I was told to try to go to sleep. The thought of sleeping with 50 electrodes attached to my head made me laugh, especially after experiencing the epilepsy disco test, but I eventually got there. Sure enough, the analyst picked up some strange brain patterns that would indicate that I had developed late-onset epilepsy. This meant I would more than likely be a medicated epileptic for the rest of my life. Two gigantic purple Epilim pills a day forever sounded easy enough and no problem at all, but what absolutely devastated me was that I couldn't play rugby for the rest of the year and couldn't work as a surf lifeguard.

At the time, those pursuits were the biggest and most important activities in my life. Mum was also a bit upset to hear that I also wasn't allowed to drive a car for a year and she would have to do more than a bit of extra driving. Everything I had planned for the next six months had to change; I had to find new work for the summer and also a new and slightly more passive sport to take up my time, preferably close to home so I wouldn't need to travel far. I let Surf Lifesaving know about the situation and they were fantastic at finding me more passive roles such as Beach Education for schools, talking to kids about being safe in the surf and helping out at youth leadership camps, which all contributed a bit of income for the summer.

I took the medication and as time passed I would slowly convince myself that perhaps I had grown out of the epilepsy and would ignorantly and secretly wean myself off the medication and try to live life as a non-epileptic.

Each time it eventually resulted in another tonic-clonic seizure, completely wiping me out for a couple of days and all due to my own stubbornness. I guess I thought there was a problem with being an epileptic and it wasn't until I came to terms with the fact that epilepsy is just a small facet of my life I need to manage that I was able to get myself over it.

I finally accepted that I was fine. Although disheartened at times by the fact that some aspects of my life had to adjust to accommodate the epilepsy, I eventually made the decision not to let it affect my enthusiasm for getting out and getting stuck into anything I wanted to do. I suppose you could say I conducted a personal vendetta against the illness and decided never to let it affect my attitude towards life or stop me from attempting different things. I figured as long as I took my medication I was no different from anyone else and I would continue living life as I did before epilepsy.

Now before you go and accuse me of vibrating my way across the Tasman, I am a well-medicated and controlled epileptic. Epilepsy was an element of my expedition that needed managing and it certainly plagued my mind in all the planning and preparation. One small seizure would be all it would take and I would be in the drink. I had only ever had three big seizures — ones lasting more than four minutes — but that is more than enough time to fall overboard and drown. This was what my family worried about most while I was crossing the ditch, always wondering if I was taking my little purple pills. I had kept the fact I was epileptic very quiet in my preparation for the crossing, only discussing it with Mum, my girlfriend Lisa and my doctor. They were all confident I would be fine as long as I took my medication religiously and took a little more when I was deprived of sleep or dehydrated, both situations linked to setting off my seizures. I'd had no sign of epileptic symptoms for about two years, but six months before departure the worst happened.

After a fairly stressed and full-on week training and boat building I woke up at Lisa's flat and had a seizure. Basically, I had let myself down by neglecting to take my medication for the whole week. Blame it on being excited about finally being able to build my boat, but I had run out of medication and hadn't made time to collect my prescription. I suppose one of the upsides of a seizure is it does provide a good talking point, as it usually occurs in the most awkward of situations. This one was no different.

The small three-bedroom Ponsonby flat was filled with some strange moans and groans as I started my seizure. Before poor Lisa had a chance to work out what was wrong, she found herself in a headlock with my arm under her pillow and her stuck in my epileptic grasp as my muscles froze. She managed to wriggle free before calling out for help. Catherine, one of her flatmates, came to the rescue. I only fitted for a few minutes, and when I woke up I took a few moments to gather my thoughts, with my usual complete loss of short-term memory. Lisa took advantage of the opportunity to try to fool me into thinking I had proposed to her!

Mum and my brother were on their way round and I knew that everyone was going to be thinking the same thing. Should I be going ahead with the Tasman crossing?

My recovery from the seizure was fine but it certainly drove home, with a new sense of fear, that I actually had no control if I didn't take my medication religiously. We had a few conversations about how I would manage the epilepsy, and I sought independent advice from a few doctors about using some other medication but was told I was using the best and just needed to ensure I took it regularly.

When it came to packing all the food for the expedition Lisa and my team of friends who came to Coffs Harbour helped me split up my medication into every food bag. Each day I was rowing I would incorporate my medication with breakfast and a couple of multivitamins. Thankfully, even at the hardest of times on the Tasman when I was at my most tired, the epilepsy didn't affect me and I was able to get on with the expedition with faith in my medication routine.

4 Surf-lifesaving adventures

After deciding to leave the school rowing club I was a bit disappointed, as I was really enjoying the racing. In hindsight this was one of the best things that could have happened, as I now needed something to fill in some time. As surf lifesaving appeared on the horizon I was introduced to the world of surfboat racing. Surfboat rowing is, to my mind, one of the greatest and most adrenaline-filled sports in the world. In most surf clubs around Australia and New Zealand, they tell an old yarn about the selection process for surfboat rowers. According to legend, all the men in the club are lined up against a wall and the sweep (usually a coach and also the guy who steers the boat) throws a brick at the wall. The men who don't move are selected for the club boat crew — obviously a bunch of surfboaties blowing their own trumpet telling this story, but nonetheless it provides an insight into the surfboat rowers' world. Thankfully, Mairangi Bay Surf Club did not employ this selection process — in fact there was no selection process. Nor was there a junior boat crew.

One day as I was lifeguarding down at Mairangi Bay I watched a bunch of blokes drag this old black wooden boat named *Bollux* onto the beach. They headed down the beach, climbed in and started rowing out into the Hauraki Gulf. I watched these guys get in using what's known as a jump start, where a surfboat rower will launch from the water and his feet land perfectly on the foot block for an explosive first stroke of the oars. After the start the blokes rowed out, smashing through small waves, and turned around a marker buoy to catch a nice tidy wave all the way back to the beach. I was hooked, I loved it and I couldn't wait to get a junior crew together for the coming season. Over the next few months I phoned around a few of my mates who were interested, but none of them were lifeguards, which was a prerequisite if you wanted to race surfboats.

From my earlier water polo playing days I knew a couple of guys from the surf club who I thought could be interested in getting into a boat and I also had my mate from school, Chris Haig, who joined the surf club with me.

After a bit of encouragement I managed to get the guys together and down for training with 'Wok', a long-time lifeguard and Speedo advocate. Wok was an old master sweep. For those of you who don't already know, a sweep is the bloke at the back of a surfboat who is in charge of the direction of the craft and takes control of the boat when it is surfing down waves. A race can be won or lost depending on the skill of the sweep and no sweep means no training, so they're an integral part of every surfboat crew.

Wok climbed into the boat and started telling us we were wearing our Speedos wrong and we needed to lube our backsides. We all sat there with suspicious looks on our face. Was he taking the piss or what? Very calmly Wok explained we should have brought our own bum cream, which led to a fairly interesting display from Wok on how one would apply bum cream and a bit of piss taking on our part.

What then followed was a solid lesson on the effects of not using bum cream (aqueous cream). As we rowed out, learning

33

how to row in time and following the person in front, the salt water on our seats began to dry. With each stroke there would be a chorus of squeaking sounds as our bums slid up and down on the plastic seats. Eventually, and inevitably, this sliding would lead to intense pain as your bum gripped the plastic and slowly turned your backside into a collection of small blisters and chaffed skin. No one wanted to be the first to stop so we all continued rowing, completely ruining ourselves for future roles as bum models and slowly learning why it was imperative to lube up and pull your Speedos up your bum before you started.

Our next training was much more successful and I began to notice that none of the guys would complain about training or equipment — instead it was all about hopping in the boat and getting stuck into a good session and catching a few good waves. Over the next few months, as we started to row in time, it became obvious to me that there was some solid potential in the crew and we might be able to give competing a try.

The day finally came when we were driving up to Waipu for our first carnival as surfboat rowers — very excited and all a bit nervous. We rocked up on Waipu Beach and started to eye up the competition and also analyse the beach and waves. A beautiful two-foot wave was running, which would certainly make for a little bit of a surf in to the beach and add some excitement.

Our first race was in about 20 minutes. We had been watching the other events during the day and the excitement was brewing. Soon enough, it was time to race and we cracked into it like pros — Speedos up our bum, all lubed up and, as the start gun fired, swearing at each other to pull harder. We pulled harder with the noise dwindling off as we became more and more tired. We swung the boat around the buoy and all started praying for a wave in to the beach. Sure enough, we got one and won our first ever surfboat race.

We would end up winning all our races and claiming the gold medal for the under-19s Auckland champs. Our crew would go on and have a great season, winning silver in the North Island surfboat champs and eventually bronze in the New Zealand Nationals. For a novice under-19s crew, this was a fairly good effort, in my books.

As I spent more time in the boat and we would head out to sea for training I began to think about ocean rowing and started to use Dad's Tasman crossing as personal motivation to get through hard sessions, always saying to myself, 'Don't be soft Quincey, Dad rowed the bloody Tasman.' Surprisingly, this would entice me to train harder and longer and certainly provided an edge of determination and drive to never give up. It was an interesting experience visiting Dad's trip in my head and using it as motivation. I'd never done this before in about 15 years of playing sport — it wasn't until I was out at sea rowing that a small seed of possibility was planted that maybe I could be the next person to row the Tasman. These thoughts would come and go and I really didn't think that much of them, but I would always catch myself researching ocean rowing expeditions and history, always wondering if I had what it took to row an ocean.

For the next six years surfboat rowing ruled my life and the sport slowly grew in both my local club and at a national level, with the number of crews competing increasing every year. In 2004 I was fortunate enough to be approached by two very competent rowers, Scott Hunter and Carl Anderson, who asked how they could be involved with surfboat rowing. At the time I was training with two other guys, Cameron Allison and Matthew Lumsden, and we were looking for one more rower to begin our campaign for our first year competing in under-21s. With five rowers and only four seats in the boat we had a slight problem. I could see how the two pairs would make a brilliant crew because of their mutually aggressive and stubborn natures but there would be no way any of them would swap around seats during the season and I could also see the crew falling apart if the boys let their temperament get the better of them. I decided rather than missing out on what could be a national title-winning crew, I would learn to sweep and in essence become the sweep/coach/manager of the under-21 Mairangi Bay surfboat crew. Slightly disappointed at not being able to row, I was also bloody nervous, as I would be in control of a great crew who would let me know if I didn't keep them straight on a wave. In what was a massive learning curve, I eventually managed to sweep the boat. Although the crew are all good friends now, the tension that developed over that year was intense, with the crew almost folding a number of times.

This was my first introduction to managing team dynamics and I began to understand that this crew could be almost invincible if I could harness the energy the pairs spent niggling each other in training sessions and play them off against each other. This worked extremely well and I would make direct statements about one rower being more effective than the other during a hard session. It was a very fine line to walk as the focus needed to be on rowing effectively and not on beating the other guy, getting the guys to use their aggression to pull harder and stay focused. The worst result the crew got that year was a silver, which was my fault. I broached on a wave out of the arena, which resulted in a dead last finish in a best-out-of-three race competition.

We won nationals and for me this was a huge relief — no more tantrums and no more liaising. I knew I would never get the guys in a crew again so that national title would be the last for them, and probably me, for some time. I would miss the off-the-water crew antics. The night after nationals was certainly one to remember, especially after a few hours in the pub on the horse racing machine pretending to be the first to take Phar Lap over the line. Of course the guys were nude, albeit in the middle of a pub filled with around 400 or so surf lifeguards, absolutely going for it riding a mechanical horse. Later that evening one of the boys thought it would be a good idea to take the floor cleaning machine from the store next door to the pub back to the hotel to start cleaning the floors of unsuspecting hotel patrons at three o'clock in the morning. Incredibly funny we thought, and it seemed like a brilliant idea at the time. Sure enough there was an early-morning visit to the police station to retrieve a crew member after he was responsible for tearing a hole in the carpet after storming into a room of some unsuspecting junior lifeguards and starting the floor polisher.

I spent the next four years racing socially, winning the odd silver or bronze medal, with off-the-oar antics probably being my focus of surf carnivals. To be honest, I was always much more excited about the night after the surfboat racing than the event itself.

Whether it was nude beach runs or kangaroo court sessions run by senior rowers, Mairangi Bay Surf Club was certainly a social sieve for shy and reclusive personalities. After each surf club event the anticipation would begin to brew about what punishment was going to be dealt to which person for something they had done during the season. Whether it was arriving late for training or breaking equipment, if you had done something stupid you would be punished. The lists of punishments would be horrendous and I recall having to scull a drink mixed with tuna chunks, milk and a tablespoon of Tabasco sauce, then having to do a run around a swimming pool in a G-string. I'm not quite sure if the run was part of the punishment or not but I will never forget those kangaroo court sessions and seeing the look of absolute despair as a punishment was handed down to a fellow clubbie.

Sadly, the world is changing and the level of these antics has certainly toned down, but for me those days were by far the most educational and character-building of my life ... and a bucketload of fun.

5   Cut the cord and attack the dream

I am lying here braced with my feet against the walls of the cabin and back against another wall, sweating and trying to eat some cold porridge. I touch a picture on the wall, remembering home. Stay positive! I remind myself it will all be worth it when I hit the shore in New Zealand. I have food and I have water but as for a strong enough mind, I'm still unsure. I have to keep reminding myself that the sea doesn't have a personal agenda to kill me or ruin my day. It's just a matter of time and I can beat it if I hold on. Fighting against it will do nothing — I am officially redundant until the invincible bully out there drops its guard and I can row again.

I still wonder how I got across that bloody ditch and how I survived some of those never-ending nights of absolute chaos. Thinking back to those times in the cabin still upsets me and fills me with feelings of sheer uselessness. I remember sitting in the cabin, the walls wet, as was all my bedding. I couldn't for the life of me figure out what was good about this trip or why I had ever thought it would be a good thing to do. I was bored, my hands were ripped up, my bum was killing me with pressure sores, I was soaked through and I hadn't slept for more than two hours at any one time.

What on earth was I thinking, back in November 2008, when

I made the decision to attempt the crossing? What made me feel I could do it when only a year ago a man died trying to achieve the exact same thing?

I've always been fairly determined and even stubborn once I eventually set my mind to something — the problem has always been what that something is going to be. Leading up to the decision I had spent two years watching my second step-father die of cancer, which was a huge eye opener. Along with his death I experienced a paradigm shift as to what I valued and what was important. Over a couple of days I realized my current job was no longer relevant to the life I wanted to lead. I started looking for an alternative immediately and got a bit frantic about it.

I looked at what I'd done so far with my life. I'd enjoyed operating my small advertising business with the coffee cups, and I'd really enjoyed working for Surf Life Saving New Zealand. I'd also studied sales and commercial law, and part of me wanted to apply those skills, but after scrolling through hundreds of jobs I couldn't help but think they all seemed boring, with no challenge for me. I knew I needed a huge change, which would challenge me in every way — business skills, physical training and creativity — something that would do justice to my life, my time and push me very hard.

At around the same time I left my job my six-year-old cousin died in a terrible accident, falling out of a golf buggy and knocking his head. I figured I'd just been through my step-father's funeral and felt fairly capable of helping out and being able to deal with death, so I jumped on a plane over to Australia to Joshua's funeral.

I'd been to a few funerals in my time but nothing prepares you for a child's funeral. Absolute despair and a great sense of unfairness surrounded the event, everybody digging hopelessly for something positive to say. Joshua's funeral cemented my desire to do something meaningful with my time and over the next couple of days I decided to head up to Darwin to catch up with Dad for the first time in 18 months.

I arrived at around midnight. Stepping off the plane I couldn't help but feel overwhelmed, going from a fairly horrific funeral straight up to Darwin to meet Dad's new wife and catch up with him for the first time in ages.

I needn't have worried — after all, it was nothing that a few beers and a solid debrief session wouldn't fix. Going to bed that night I realized I had absolutely no idea of what Darwin had to offer and what I could get up to while I was there. It was also at this time that it really started to dawn on me that I had a burning desire to row the Tasman Sea.

Unlike other outlandish plans and alcohol-fuelled pipe dreams I'd had before, this one had floated in my head for years. I'd only ever told one very close friend, Michael Buck, that some day I would love to row the Tasman. Funnily enough, he ended up being my land manager for the expedition. Even though I was in Darwin and had possibly one of the best Tasman Sea resources available to me — after all, my father was the only person to have ever rowed the ditch single-handed — at that point I wasn't ready to approach him. I knew I needed to plan and research the project first. I had a huge amount of respect for what he had achieved and felt that I needed to do the work and research and plan it all first to show I was serious, before I started to question him about his experiences. So during my time over in Darwin I flicked the odd question to him about the Tasman, but we spent most of our time touring the crocodile-ridden sweaty mecca of tropical Darwin.

I spent a week with Dad and Nitaya, his wife, constantly thinking about the Tasman and trying to figure out if my personality and nature matched Dad's enough to be able to do what he had done, wondering if I would have the ability to complete the crossing. Am I mentally strong enough? I would ask myself over and over again. I always knew I was physically strong enough, after racing surfboats, but the Tasman would take me into a new realm of challenge. I wanted to know if I had enough of my father's traits in me to get across the ditch.

We were completely different physically. Dad was as skinny as a rake while I'd played rugby as a prop for 18 years, trying to be as big, heavy and strong as possible. Not to mention possibly a few too many trips to local bakeries never really working in my favour. We were certainly polar opposites in our physical make-up, but that didn't really worry me as I thought having a bit of extra meat on the bone would probably be an advantage in the long run.

I have a massive and unreasonable fear of flying so I tend to inebriate myself in one way or another as my usual method of dealing with it. I try to have enough beer and whisky before the flight to make sure I either sleep through it or, even better, not even realize I am flying! Coming back home from Darwin was no different, and I ended up spending nine hours in Brisbane Airport, very hung over, waiting for a connecting flight to Auckland. As I sweated out the beer from the night before I whipped out my laptop and started to draft a budget for a potential Tasman crossing. This certainly didn't help the hangover, especially when comparing my current personal balance sheet with what I would require over the next few years.

I guess this would have been the real beginning of the campaign. I had certainly made the decision, but it was very far from a reality as what I had just worked out showed me I needed to find around $85,000 whereas the assets of a 24-year-old student came to one 32-inch flat-screen TV and a drum kit.

The creative juices started to flow about how I was going to raise the capital I needed, and the *Tasman Trespasser II* campaign had begun, all while I was sitting and sweating on a dusty floor at Brisbane Airport.

I arrived back in Auckland after a terrifying flight (as usual) and was picked up by my girlfriend of one and a bit months, Lisa Jones. I didn't think it wise at the time to inform her of the plan to row across the Tasman, as we were still working through a wee incident from a few weeks prior.

I had celebrated my 24th birthday, which is usually a fairly standard event — unless your new and potential long-term girlfriend thinks you're turning 27 … a minor issue in my books but this did take some fairly serious damage control after confessing at midnight before my birthday that she was actually dating someone a little bit younger than she thought.

I wasn't ready to announce my plans. I needed more credibility and I needed to do more research, after spending a couple of days at work exploiting an Internet account with extensive searches on Tasman Sea conditions and ocean rowing.

I decided this would not be the place for me while preparing for the crossing and I ended up leaving the good job, the work car and the work phone within a few weeks. The Tasman had to be taken seriously and I had to approach my campaign seriously and professionally. This would mean giving up everything I had in order to make the expedition happen. I had hundreds and hundreds of questions and a fair idea of who I could ask to get some answers, but sooner or later I would have to announce to the world that I was taking on this challenge, which was going to be a task in itself.

How on earth do I tell everyone I'm going to row the Tasman Sea? More importantly, how do I tell everyone and maintain some level of respect? I'd been studying for a Bachelor of Business degree and rowing the Tasman certainly isn't the path I think Mum expected me to pursue. I was doing quite well as far as she was concerned, all the basics were covered — a job, a nice new girlfriend and a great bunch of mates in a new flat all cruising along quite happily.

When the time came to announce to the world that I was going to take on the Tasman I was quite nervous about how to approach it and how exactly this would play out. Many different thoughts were in my head about people's reactions. Would people try to stop me? Would they think I'm crazy? Do I need to tell the authorities first? So many questions, and again without a guiding mentor, I decided to rely on instinct. I thought it best to tell Dad first; he would obviously be an integral aspect of the expedition and deserved to know before anyone else. I decided to let him know in an email, which would give me time to think about exactly how I would word it.

Hi Dad

I completed an ocean swim on the weekend, 3 km from Bayswater wharf to the Viaduct Marina. Took me 56 min. Was kind of happy with that but not really, could have gone under 50 min I believe but oh well.

Anyway this little adventure has stirred a huge sense of adventure in me and I now realize how immensely bored I am with the Rat Race etc. People are meant to do more than work and I think it is what you do out of work that defines you.

44

... so I have decided to have a crack at the Tasman and follow in my greatest role model's footsteps. This is something I would love you to help me with and hopefully with my knack with media and advertising experience I will be able to fly you over to help out with some of the planning etc — this isn't a spur of the moment decision, this has plagued my mind since I started surfboat rowing at least six years ago and I have a few funding plans and sponsorship etc. With my research on weather and trade currents etc I plan to leave a year from today. ETD = November 20th 2009 from Sydney to New Zealand, landing somewhere on the North Island west coast.

What are your thoughts? I need help with basic ocean knowledge, navigation, fitness and rowing easy, nutrition. I can get boat construction sorted. I am currently writing a letter to Salthouse brothers as they helped you so will see what I can negotiate with them. I have a design, I plan to buy the plans and get the boat shipped to Australia after NZ testing. Plans are Solo ocean crosser, designed by Woodvale, build hopefully Kevlar carbon fibre, bulletproof and light.

Should keep me busy for a year :-)

What are your thoughts? (Don't tell Ben or Mum yet until I have some more plans in place then I want Ben involved but probably better if Mum stays out for a while until a few things are sorted.)

I have never been happier than now with a plan like this on the go !!!!!!! Life is great, I have taken your situation in Darwin into consideration and understand your commitments there so no pressure, just would love it if you were involved.

Shaun Quincey — Tasman Trespasser II skipper

Dad's first reply to me was a simple email, which said:

That's a good idea
More to come next 24 hours
Love Dad

I wasn't really surprised by Dad's brief reply; I knew the news would come to him as a bit of a shock, as I had never indicated I was interested in attempting the Tasman, and being Dad, he'd want to give it some thought.

His response after 24 hours went as follows:

Hi Shaun,

You have my <u>unreserved</u> support, or as Nike say — JUST DO IT!
Tell me a good time to call you this weekend.
For now — you have addressed the most simple question of life, 'what matters?' and come up with the correct answer.

Another great response, which filled me with enthusiasm and provided more motivation to continue down the path I had chosen. I guess I'll always wonder if I would have gone ahead if he had said it was a bad idea, not that he really had a foot to stand on. I decided to wait to tell everyone else until after I had spoken to Dad on the weekend to get a better understanding of his thoughts. It was hard for me to keep it to myself, as I was very excited about the expedition.

Dad gave me a call and I went through with him what I'd been thinking and told him what research I had completed so far and exactly what I was planning to do. I could tell immediately that all the Tasman talk was stirring up excitement within him and I got to see the adventurer side of Dad, which I hadn't seen for a long time — almost instantly confirming I was heading down the right track. The conversation ended with Dad saying it was incredibly important I conduct all of my own research and preparation and I wasn't to rely on his experience or knowledge, because so much of the technology and safety had changed. I was on a high — I now had the support of the only other person to have crossed the Tasman, and all I had to do now was tell all the other important people in my life. The next would have to be Mum and I decided to do this with a phone call and allocate a solid few hours to field all her questions and calm her nerves.

Mum surprised me and actually took it really well. I couldn't believe it — my entire rugby-playing life I'd had to fight to be able to play because she hated the game. I thought telling her about the Tasman would be another major battle, but when the words 'If that's what you want to do then I will support you' came out of her mouth I was very surprised. Now I had ticked two out of the three major boxes, with the last being Lisa.

Her involvement would be key to both the project and our relationship. I knew that if she didn't like the idea of me rowing the Tasman, the prospects of a future relationship were slim to none. First I told Lisa I had left my job and she was rapt, because she knew how much I hated it and subsequently I was hit with:

'So what are you going to do now?'

'Well, I think I'm going to row the Tasman.

'I know.'

'What do you mean you know?' I immediately thought Mum had called her. 'Who told you!?'

'You did.'

Now I was definitely confused.

Lisa explained that on the night of my 24th birthday, after a day of fishing and drinking a few too many beers, I announced I was going to row the Tasman and that if she wanted to stay with me she had to know I would be doing this. This was a surprise to me but fantastic that I had her support. At the time I had no idea exactly how important having Lisa was going to be in getting through the next 15 months.

Next came my brother Ben. We'd both grown up with the same stories of our father rowing the Tasman and I believe there was a small fire in him to do something similar. My initial idea was to approach Ben about a two-man crossing, but after thinking about this for some time I steered away from the idea. It was the wrong time. His priority was now his family, and he had just recently become engaged to Megan (now his wife) and I didn't think she'd have a bar of Ben rowing the Tasman. When I called Ben to let him know I was going to give it a crack he was enthusiastic.

Now that I'd told the important people about what I was doing and had their support, my main focus was figuring out how I go about not letting them down. I needed to start talking to the right people about how to put a framework in place to make *Tasman Trespasser II* a reality.

6   Team Tasman

As well as what seemed like all of the North Shore, I had been personally in contact with everyone important who needed to be told I was attempting to row the Tasman.

It was a very interesting feeling, having announced I was on this massive mission and trying to figure out where on earth to start — and what starting even involved. Typical of my generation, I jumped on the Internet to start exploring ocean rowers and tried to find out how they had started.

Fortunately for me, there are now a few ocean rowers around and lots of information has been collected in and around the history and sport of ocean rowing. There was even an ocean rowing society website to visit for information. I spent hours researching the fundamentals and started writing lists about what types of equipment people used, how they used it and also what levels of support they'd been able to obtain and how much money it had cost.

The most recent expedition was the 'Crossing the Ditch' campaign run by two Australian guys the same age as me, who had paddled the first double kayak across the Tasman. It was obvious to me that the guys were very capable and savvy, with the way their website had been constructed and the manner in which they had managed and organized their crossing. Researching their campaign methodologies I found a number of useful contacts on their website — potential sponsors or people with an insight into how I should proceed in the early stages of organizing my campaign. Hours of research and years of experience can be saved if you're lucky enough to talk with the right person about a particular topic at the right time.

I was incredibly lucky to get in touch with a man by the name of Patrick Brothers, who was a director of a company called Rush Labs. I went to their website and completed some due diligence on exactly what his company did before deciding to give him a call at his Sydney office. I told Pat I was planning to row the Tasman, my dad was the first person to do it back in 1977 and I was looking for some support — basically advice and direction as to how to proceed.

Pat came across as interested, but also slightly apprehensive, probably because he had just finished working with the kayakers and knew what he would be in for if he agreed to help me.

After a few days I got a call from Pat, who told me that Rush Labs saw the project as worthwhile and would like to send me a proposal about what they could do to assist my expedition. At first I did find it slightly strange that Pat was keen to help — he'd never met me and only knew what I'd told him on the phone, so I was slightly dubious as I waited for his proposal.

What Pat sent through showed how he thought Rush Labs could assist me by providing me with an initial branding frame, which would be critical to developing a sponsored adventure campaign like mine. It would involve branding and website construction as well as media release strategies and a way to measure the results — all important factors if I wanted to impress upon potential sponsors that I knew what I was doing when I asked them to invest their money in my project.

After reading through the strategy I knew immediately that I wanted Pat and Rush Labs to be a part of my expedition. I was incredibly impressed by their professionalism and, although money was tight, Pat's skills and experience would hopefully open the doors to more funding down the track.

The Rush Labs crew swung into action within a few weeks and before I had much time to think about the direction I was heading in, they had designed a couple of potential websites and concept branding ideas.

With the look and feel of the campaign starting to take shape I now needed some help setting up the business entity and framework the *Tasman Trespasser II* campaign was going to operate, and I could see I was going to need some help managing this aspect.

My good friend Oliver Young was working as a business advisory accountant, so I arranged to meet him and grab a coffee to talk about what I was up to and what he thought I would need in place. Olly was great, he took responsibility for this part of the campaign and ran with it, rather than sitting back and constantly waiting for instructions. Olly came back to me with a number of possible solutions and with some help from a family friend who was a lawyer, the commercial operating side of *Tasman Trespasser II* slowly started to take form. Structures were falling into place to ensure I could operate as a commercial organization, adding much-needed professionalism to my campaign.

The plan was in place and ready to roll out. I had confidence in the resources Patrick and the Rush Labs team had helped to create and the website was looking good. Even though I'd still made no real tangible steps towards obtaining a boat, I'd been given a stage to launch from and the ball was definitely rolling. Salthouse Boatbuilders were locked in and ready to provide the space to build *TTII* and with the website up and running I could slowly begin to see things coming together.

The reality of life was kicking in at this stage, with cell phone bills and rent due. The horrible normality of having to pay these bills was definitely hitting home and making the prospect of raising sponsorship seem just that much harder. Constantly on my mind was the purchase of the kitset boat from WoodVale Ocean Rowing — a $12,500 compulsory cost and I had no idea where it was coming from.

Each day sitting at my computer, researching either the Tasman Sea or ocean rowing, I would phone companies to propose a commercial sponsorship, happily directing them to the new website. This was great to have, as it gave me credibility, but certainly wouldn't close the deal. I needed an injection of cash as soon as possible, preferably around $15,000 to keep the project wheels spinning.

I would sit at the computer, lost in thought about how to raise money, increasingly concerned about all the work Olly and Pat had already done, knowing I had a great set of tools to start the project moving. I was now facing my biggest hurdle so far. Where were the people who would support me financially and how exactly was I going to create a community of supporters to help push me along? The Internet was a fantastic tool, providing forums such as Facebook and Twitter, which I used to gather support, let people know what I was doing and provide forums to connect with other ocean rowers and potential sponsors.

Ten months out from departure date and what had been achieved? My family had been informed and I had a framework to support media involvement but I still had no boat and no money. I decided it was time to try to involve the media, and hopefully generate a bit of interest in what I was up to. While I knew I needed to do it, a part of me was a bit apprehensive about telling the media when I still didn't have any real backers. To tell the truth, I was very unsure about how it was going to happen and didn't have answers to many of the questions common sense told me I would be asked.

Nervously, I called the local news paper, the *North Shore Times*, and left a message telling them I was rowing the Tasman solo and needed some support. No one called back.

I was genuinely shocked. Surely, my story had some credibility — this was something that had never been done before, rowing the Tasman solo from west to east, my Dad is the only other person to have rowed the Tasman solo, and, damn it, I'm from the North Shore! Why weren't they interested?

When two days had gone by without any answer I was so disgruntled I borrowed my flatmate's bike and took off down to the head office of the *North Shore Times*, where I asked to see the editor. Unfortunately for me, the editor wasn't in the office that day, but I did get the opportunity to meet Hayden Donnell, one of the reporters.

He was interested and told me to email the *North Shore Times* with a press release. He also suggested a time to meet at my father's boat, *Tasman Trespasser*, which was on display at the Auckland Maritime Museum, for a photoshoot. Brilliant — this was exactly what I had hoped would happen.

The photoshoot was painless and over within 30 minutes. I sat down next to Dad's boat with the reporter and the dreaded questions began. 'Shaun, when is the boat going to be finished?' followed by 'When will you be departing?' and of course 'Who's your support crew?' I didn't have a definite answer to any of the questions, and any answer I did give was always going to be subject to change. Not that I was going to let that get in my way. I managed to supply him with answers based around the fail-safe method of guessing when things should be done.

Overall I felt my first interview had gone well and I managed to get the reporter to add that I was looking for sponsors and needed as much help as possible. The paper with my story was due out on the Thursday and I found myself reading the Tuesday paper and feeling envious of the different stories, and wondering why they were getting coverage so easily when I'd had to work so hard to get mine. When I realized what it actually was I laughed at my own media-coverage envy and waited patiently for Thursday.

Holy hell! There I was on the front page, standing next to my father's boat telling the entire North Shore of Auckland how I was going to row across the Tasman. Totally happy with the result of my first foray into the media for the campaign, I was sure I'd now be able to start hunting down some sponsorship.

As the project continued and I became more familiar with press releases and the media, I learned to compare my story with what else was currently in the news. My next big lesson in reality came when I did my first national release to major newspapers and general media, and had very little response. To be precise, out of around 250 media outlets I received two responses — every other paper or television station was entirely focused on the recession and its effects. I remember wondering to myself what had happened to New Zealand. Why on earth are we so negative all the time?

Realizing I needed to make some more sacrifices to show supporters and prove to myself I was willing to give the Tasman a fair shot, I phoned my brother asking if I could set up a bedroom in his garage attic to try to save some money.

While people I'd told about my plan to row the Tasman were supportive, this support wasn't turning into financial sponsorship, which I still desperately needed. I felt as though I was alone in the bottom of an offal pit; no one shared my passion and every potential sponsor I called didn't want to know me.

As Ben was getting married, Dad was due over for a visit in the next few weeks. With the Tasman plaguing my mind I needed to think of a way to utilize Dad's time here to leverage as much media coverage as possible, while also bearing in mind that Dad wasn't the biggest fan of being in front of the media.

7 Lacks experience but full of enthusiasm

In what seemed at the time like endless banter about the expedition with various salty sea dogs around Auckland, I was subjected to a constant barrage of sailor talk and worrisome sea-going tales and was heavily questioned on technical aspects of the expedition I was planning. I couldn't answer most of the questions. Having never been to sea before, as in never out of sight of land, it dawned on me that two serious weaknesses were my huge lack of ocean-going experience and any sort of technical knowledge.

With the pressure of time constantly against me I needed to dramatically increase my maritime knowledge. I drew up a list of areas where I lacked the essential know-how to get from point A to point B, in a boat at sea. I also started to investigate whether there were any international standards for rowing a boat from Australia to New Zealand. Were there any qualifications I might need?

I found guidelines scattered around various web pages, all of which seemed to cover off the basic equipment items such as EPIRB (Emergency Position Indicating Radio Beacon), life raft and short-range radios, but there didn't seem to be any indication of qualifications or experience. I was confident I could handle the big seas and being tossed around in a small boat, after all I'd already experienced that with surfboat rowing. What I was afraid of was my expedition being postponed or disallowed because of some legislative anomaly that would lead to some sort of governing body deciding it wasn't a good idea.

My way of dealing with this was to actively engage all of the authorities I assumed would take an interest in what I was doing, so I emailed or wrote letters to Australian and New Zealand Search and Rescue, Australian and New Zealand Maritime Safety Authorities, Australian Customs, New South Wales Police and New South Wales Coast Guard.

I asked all of them for feedback on compulsory equipment I should have on board and what sort of experience, as well as qualifications, they would expect me to have in order to row from Australia to New Zealand. It was a huge relief, after all my worrying and concern, that I didn't get a single negative reply or damning suggestion of not being allowed to depart Australian shores. I was pleasantly surprised to find that I didn't really need much training or qualifications, and as long as I had the correct equipment I could basically row where I wanted.

The next box I needed to tick was navigation, with visions of rocking side to side trying to obtain a sextant reading, as my father had. I had a fairly misconstrued idea of what ocean navigation might entail and I was also slightly embarrassed to ask for help, as I thought most people would assume I was already a highly proficient navigator, seeing as though I was about to embark on rowing across an ocean in a few months.

But this wasn't the case and I was the absolute definition of an amateur, with no idea how to navigate. Put it this way: my risk-management plan was to row away from the sunset each night, this being west — where could I possibly go wrong? Clearly, some work needed to be done in this area and I enrolled in a sea survival course and read a number of celestial navigation books, which filled the gaps rather rapidly and provided a collection of skills to draw upon.

Slowly, as the months went by it became very obvious I wasn't going to be venturing out into the Hauraki Gulf on an overnight expedition to test my new knowledge — there just wasn't time. Whenever a gap in the clouds did appear, I either had hurt myself training or had booked in some other equally essential component of my preparation.

Instead I was going to have to get in the boat whenever I could and practise the routines I would be using when I was out on the Tasman. Whether I could fit in 30 minutes' or three hours' rowing, I would just have to do my best to simulate conditions and routines as best I could.

As I was slowly ticking the boxes for what I needed to learn and prepare for, I booked in for a sea survival course in Auckland, which involved some heavy theory on navigation and course plotting, as well as emergency procedures, before we were allowed to play in a life raft. I had basically taught myself most of the theory before the course so it was great for reinforcing what I'd learnt. As the day went on I was hanging out to set off the life raft in the wave pool and get a bit of practical experience under my belt.

When the time came I jumped in the water in full wet-weather gear and the auto inflate mechanism on my lifejacket immediately went off. As planned, the instructor started to blast me in the eyes with a fire hose, annoying as hell, but to be fair I would do exactly the same if I was running the course. The next step was to scramble into the life raft as it was being thrown around the wave pool and attempt to bail it out. I flopped in and the stench of freshly glued rubber was the first thing I noticed — it was suffocating in the closed environment. The waves were really throwing the raft around, so my next task was to flip it upside down and then try to right the raft. As I was being flipped around and submerged inside the life raft I made the decision that climbing into a raft was going to be the very last possible resort for me if I got into trouble.

Before the course I'd imagined a life raft would be like a big, comfortable lilo and the thought of leaving my boat and climbing into one hadn't seemed like a big deal. With this serious misconception dissolved I decided I'd be sticking to *TTII* until the bitter end.

As I learnt more about ocean navigation and risk management at sea, my confidence in my ability to deal with situations I might face slowly grew. I started to compile a notebook of possible risks I might face out on the Tasman and exactly how I would deal with each of them. As I started to break down the components of potentially life-threatening situations, I saw how each one could be mitigated and the risks substantially minimized. With my knowledge of sea survival and safety slowly coming along I started to feel less ignorant when people asked me what would happen if I sank. It dawned on me that the most annoying part about rowing an ocean solo was having to know everything myself. The more I was learning, the more I would see massive gaps in my knowledge.

The weather was obviously going to play a huge role while I was out on the ditch and understanding it would provide an insight into exactly what I was in for — the Tasman has been described as the worst place a sailor could possible sail, famous for being terribly unpredictable. To try to get a handle on what that meant, I scanned through about 50 old Sydney to Hobart race videos, and saw for myself how some of the waves made 60-foot yachts look like Matchbox toys. If things went to plan I would be on the Tasman at around the same time of year as the Sydney to Hobart and could expect to experience some of the same conditions.

I asked Dad a few questions about the type of weather to expect and how big the waves actually get. He replied that it doesn't really matter how big the waves are, it's more about how steep and whether they're breaking, telling me that a 2 m breaking wave is far more treacherous than a 15 m swell.

In researching the Tasman and which direction waves come from and how they're generated, I learned that how big waves will be and how fast they will be moving are dictated by a combination of wind speed and duration.

With this in mind I figured out that the best time to row the Tasman is when it's not very windy, but when on earth was that? I managed to track down the past 15 years of weather reports, which gave me exact wind speeds and directions and from this I was able to average out when there was the most wind and when it was most likely to be blowing in the correct direction.

The general trends indicated November or December would be the best time to leave, with a predominant westerly trend, moving more to easterly winds towards the end of January. The troubling part about the Tasman weather statistics I found was that every single year there was a storm somewhere on the Tasman almost every single week, ranging from 30-knot stiff breezes to 80-plus-knot gales. Along with these storms would be 5 m waves, a lot of which would be breaking onto me and my boat.

Being ignorant of exactly what it was going to be like rowing in those sorts of conditions was more than likely my saving grace, as I was to find out for myself the adversity these storms inevitably bring and the mental fatigue you go through when one of them blows you backwards more than 90 km in one day.

The reality was that I was going to be thrown into a few of these storms, but I was sure some of them would blow me towards New Zealand, as well as away from it. As long as I did everything I could to speed the boat up in the right direction and everything I could to slow the boat down when it was going in the wrong direction, I would eventually make progress in the right direction. Simple. Yes, I was that naive then.

My conclusion about the weather was that basically there was no perfect time to cross the Tasman, the only guarantee being that there would be plenty of storms along the way and I would certainly be blown backwards a lot.

My basic analysis of the Tasman being generally rubbish was reinforced by Rodger Badham, the world-class meteorologist I would eventually rely on for my weather forecasting. When I asked when he thought the best time would be to cross, he initially replied, 'Never — there are bloody planes!' He then went on to say, 'The middle of summer because it's warm and there tend to be a few less tropical cyclones.'

A few less tropical cyclones sounded like a great idea, and although I had first thought I would try to depart in November I relaxed a little with the idea that maybe I might get Christmas at home and it wouldn't be too much of a drama if I left a bit later.

I like to think I relaxed about the weather but the unpredictable and unknown certainly drives curiosity. I'd watch the news most nights, checking isobar maps and log on to meteorological websites to catch a glimpse of wind speeds and wave heights in the Tasman. Again, there was no real information to help me, but it did provide an understanding of some of the possibilities and the way some of the storms moved around the ditch. Slowly, I felt as if I was ticking boxes again and gaining a small amount of confidence in my knowledge of the Tasman and my own seaworthiness.

The next challenge was understanding Tasman currents. I'd seen *Finding Nemo*, a film about a lost fish who swam down the coast of Australia. On his travels he jumped into the East Australian Current (EAC) with a bunch of turtles. The EAC was the key to the first part of the crossing, and understanding this and how to use it effectively was essential. In analysing previous failed rowing expeditions, my general assessment was that the rowers hadn't used the EAC to their best advantage.

The EAC flowed at various speeds and up to around 5 knots at its fastest. I thought the fact that it flowed around three times as fast as I could row was extremely significant. This massive amount of water flowed from the north of Australia in a general southerly direction, forming a collection of about 20 gigantic eddies of water, all of which were interlinked into each other like a collection of cogs spinning the gearbox of the ocean. The size of these pools ranged from a few kilometres to about 556 km wide, all moving in different directions. The pools could be viewed using satellite imagery and thermal imaging from space to identify where the warm and cold water was moving. Every few weeks the pools would change a small amount in position or speed, making expedition course plotting difficult in advance.

Keeping an avid eye on these currents was going to be an essential aspect of the expedition — rowing into the wrong one could certainly end the trip or lose me kilometres. The information available on the EAC was fantastic and made researching this aspect of the expedition rather simple, as I could see the best places to start from and where I could expect to eventually end up. The holes in my knowledge were slowly being filled: weather, currents, navigation, safety. I was a self-confessed amateur in all of them, being one step up from novice, but I had made a start in the areas I needed to know about. Quincey the ocean rower was starting to take shape mentally. The next void that needed filling was: what on earth am I going to bloody eat while I'm out there? How am I going to hold up physically if I end up rowing for 80 days?

Fortunately for me, Lisa had a good friend, Rebecca Yortt, who was a dietician and keen to help out in some way. I sat down with Becs and did a few basic summaries of what I was currently eating and what I was eating while I was training on the rowing machine. At this stage I hadn't completed many endurance indoor rows and the greatest distance I had covered was around 50 km in one sitting. This only took a few hours so I hadn't really tried to eat and continue rowing afterwards.

Becs started working on a plan and researched the nutritional needs of ocean rowers. While she did this, it was my job to weigh myself before and after each rowing session to estimate how much water I was losing and what I would need to replace. We worked out I was losing about 250 grams of weight per hour of rowing, with a maximum weight loss of close to 2.8 kilos if I rowed for more than five hours. After a few basic sums in my head I started to get a bit worried. If I rowed for 50 days, losing 2.8 kilos every five hours of rowing, I would completely dissolve. I suggested to Rebecca that perhaps we should work on a few strategies around this.

She came up with a hydration formula based around me checking my weight whenever I finished a row or was having a break, then replacing 150 per cent of the weight loss with water or sports drink. For example, if my weight had dropped 500 grams I needed to drink 750 millilitres of fluid — either isotonic sports drink or water. The increased fluid intake certainly helped and I lost substantially less weight. The only disadvantage was that I found myself having to go to the toilet every 30 minutes and this wasn't something I wanted to be doing as I was trying to row the Tasman. I was known for my mouse-sized bladder anyway so I tried to think of different ways to pee while rowing, especially during 6- to 10-hour rowing sessions. After a few schemes involving catheters I quickly moved on to a simple bucket.

I would eventually find a good balance of drinking electrolyte-based drink and a smaller amount of pure water, which meant I would only need to jump off the machine around every three or so hours, and my weight loss was reduced. This formula provided the basis of how much water I would need to drink on the Tasman and led to me choosing a particular type of water-maker able to produce the required amount each day.

The next step was to figure out how much and what I could eat while rowing. It was important to make sure I was able to perform physically on the limited types of food I could take and prepare. At this stage my knowledge of food for sport was fairly limited and I didn't really have the best diet to match what I was trying to achieve.

Becks asked me to start keeping a food diary so we could start to analyse how I felt on different types of food and amounts, and how that affected my physical performance. In particular we looked for any detrimental effects. We tried a variety of different foods based around high-carbohydrate and high-calorie foods. A typical trial day would start at 5 a.m. with two cups of porridge with half a cup of sultanas, a tablespoon of sugar, four spoons of carbohydrate powder and half a packet of ground almonds, which would equate to about two bowls of sticky breakfast. I would then fill all my drink bottles for the day and start on an eight-hour indoor row. After three hours I'd break for my next meal, which would usually be a quick two tins of creamed rice, a banana and some jelly lollies, then back on the machine for another couple of hours. Lunch would be a couple of huge bread rolls filled with whatever I had in the fridge, a bag of salty nuts and another banana, before hopping back on the rowing machine to finish my eight-hour stint.

Each session I experienced different results, whether it was vomiting from being too full or diarrhoea from a bad reaction to one of the foods. Eventually, we were able to eliminate what didn't work for me and I slowly became used to exercising on a very full stomach, which was one of my greatest challenges.

Rebecca played a vital role in giving me a path to follow and we figured out what I needed to perform on. This provided a great shopping list for when I eventually got enough money to start purchasing food for the trip.

While all the testing and trialling was going on I was constantly on the phone to potential sponsors and a lot of them happened to be food suppliers. Around 20 per cent of the sponsors I approached would say no to sponsoring me with cash, instead offering me goods to either use, sell or eat. Every little bit counted so I never said no to anything I could use.

On one occasion a friend knew one of the managers at Heinz Wattie's Limited, who worked in the dessert department. This guy had caught wind of what I was up to and sent me an email.

He'd heard how I was struggling a bit to find sponsorship and offered to send me a few of their products to help out. I sent back a brief thank you, not expecting much more than a few sample packs. A few days went past and there was a knock on my door from a delivery truck driver, asking me where I wanted the creamed rice.

I followed him back outside, assuming I'd be able to carry them myself. The driver rolled open the back of the truck to reveal 560 full-sized tins of Wattie's Creamed Rice. Fairly stunned at their generosity, I wondered how on earth I was going to eat my way through this many bloody tins. After an hour and a half of unpacking the tins and stacking them in my brother's garage, I had managed to build a small enclosure around the rowing machine out of creamed rice tins. To this day I still have about 150 tins sitting there.

Weather, navigation, safety, hydration, food. Check! By now it was May 2009 and I was still planning on leaving in November. Help was starting to roll in and while I knew a whole lot more about what I needed to do, I still didn't have a boat and it was time to do something about it.

8 No = 390, Yes = 2

So far I had raised $4000 through the sale of my drums and TV, which was a great start as far as I was concerned and about enough for a coat of paint and four oars — both integral but not quite enough to get the boat built, ship it to Australia and fill it with food and equipment.

I had enough motivation and drive to run a small planet at this stage, my enthusiasm fresh and not yet dulled, but the reality of living on nothing and endlessly attempting to sell sponsorship in a recession began to take its toll. In an immature and naive attempt to rustle up sponsorship I made some muddled and confused phone calls before I realized that all my motivation and drive would be completely useless until I started focusing on key initiatives. I needed to plot out a path that would eventually take me in the direction I needed to go, which was towards rowing the Tasman.

Each phone call would go along the same lines.

'Hi, my name is Shaun Quincey. In November 2010 I'll be attempting to row the Tasman from Australia to New Zealand.'

'That's great, do you have a proposal you could send through?'

'No worries!'

I would send through the proposal and usually get a generic email response, each one based around a couple of the same things. Either: *Due to the current economic climate we won't be sponsoring you*, or *We already currently sponsor another organization so won't be sponsoring you*. It didn't matter which one I got, because they both ended the same way. We won't be sponsoring you!

Understandably, I was a high-risk option for their marketing dollars and the world *was* in a financial crisis, but each rejection somehow made me even more determined to get across the ditch in spite of them. Initially, the rejection letters or emails would throw me back a bit and made me reflect on what I was doing, thinking that perhaps people just aren't all that interested. While I did my best to stay motivated and enthusiastic, each 'No' does chip a little bit away from you.

It had been three months with absolutely no significant breakthroughs — at this stage I would have contacted close to 60 companies and emailed very basic sales proposals to each of the appropriate managers who hadn't given me a direct no over the phone. I always knew I was going to attempt the crossing and had never been more serious about a particular goal, but for some reason or another I couldn't seem to convey this to the companies I was approaching.

Looking back now, I think I was still too casual and relaxed. I took myself seriously, but in hindsight I can see how I wouldn't have come across seriously to them, probably due to my generally relaxed demeanour.

The reality was that in order to raise funds I needed to become a viable option for people with commercial advertising dollars. I needed to develop a brand that businesses wanted to be associated with, and *Tasman Trespasser II* needed to offer a dynamic advertising opportunity. It was my role to construct a combination of unique and generic advertising mediums to interest potential sponsors and to do that I would have to get out there and sell my backside off!

Each day would start the same, eating a massive bowl of porridge then sitting down in front of the computer flicking through my emails, hoping one would say 'Yes we would love to sponsor you,' which of course never happened.

As I started to receive coverage through radio interviews and the odd newspaper article, I would keep these and show sponsorship targets the different media I had received and point out how they could be sharing this with me.

This was a very challenging and lonely time — with each rejection I felt my goal was moving further away. I built up so much hope with each slightly positive response, only to be let down every time. I don't think people ever realized how much I was putting into the campaign to give it credibility. Every dollar I had was poured into it — *Tasman Trespasser II* came before food. Because I believed that to achieve the ultimate goal the ultimate sacrifices had to be made, everything I had was sold. Drums, clothing, TV, basically everything I didn't need for the trip was sold.

January and February were the hardest. I actually had nothing — not a dollar. All my money had gone to refurbishing Dad's historical documents and sending out proposals. I still believe I was right to do it, though, because people will not support you until you show them you're 110 per cent committed to your cause. If I was going to ask people for money I needed to know I had put *everything* into achieving my goal.

I always knew things were ultimately going to be OK and I would get through but when you've just rowed 21 km on a rowing machine and you know there isn't any real food in the flat the creative chef certainly comes to life, and I ended up concocting all sorts of delightful meals.

Tasman Trespasser Preparation cooking lesson one
  Two cups macaroni into pot of water
  Try to light gas.
  Oops, haven't paid gas bill.
  Dilemma.
  Microwave!
  Two cups macaroni into microwave-proof plastic pot.
  Add cold water and microwave for five minutes.
  Investigate possible ingredients.
  Pantry looking a bit bare.
  Look behind the bin.
  Success! Cocoa, flour, sun-dried tomatoes, golden syrup,
    Parmesan cheese.
  Ding of microwave.
  Make executive decision as to what will join the macaroni
    in the pot.
  Add cocoa and golden syrup.

Quite a reasonable mix I thought. The issue I think most people will have is how a jar of sun-dried tomatoes went in followed by around half a cup of Parmesan cheese. Then it all went back in the microwave for five more minutes.

It was then stirred and eaten with a piece of mouldy bread — toasted of course, to kill the mould. It's amazing what you'll eat when you're hungry. I justified the meal as pasta = carbs, golden syrup = glucose, cheese and cocoa = fat ... I get stuck on the sun-dried tomatoes, which I put down to hunger and flavour. All of this was enough to get me through another 21 km row on the rowing machine. Funnily enough, the flatmates didn't help themselves, so there was enough left over for seconds after my next row.

This was how it was, scrimping and scraping for money as I slowly started to gather support. I thought about going on a benefit but would never have forgiven myself, so I hunted around for part-time work. Foolishly thinking I would have time, I applied for jobs with the mindset that they would bring in a few dollars and only be short term. I sent my CV off for all sorts of different things, such as a YMCA membership salesperson and a golf course groundskeeper. I ended up working as a hammer hand for several different builders, labouring all over the show. Labouring was great and would provide me with a bit of a workout as well as some cash. The hours were generally fairly flexible, so I paid the bills each week with two or three days labouring around Auckland.

As the weeks went by a few product sponsors started to come on board and, as each one did, it would take a small chunk off the total budget and also provide a small motivational boost to keep going. Kathmandu, the clothing company, was my first product sponsor, offering me a $5000 collection of very useful clothing, all of which I would need.

My first major win came from a phone call to James Frankham, editor of *New Zealand Geographic*. I called James thinking that perhaps the magazine would be interested in publishing a story about both Dad's and my trips. They certainly were — and even better, the New Zealand Geographic Trust was also interested in providing me with $2000 of sponsorship money, in return for access to Dad's photos as well as the story! Like a kid in a sweet shop I told them I would be straight down to show them Dad's photos and have a chat about it.

Grabbing a shirt off the floor I had it ironed and was in the car and on the way down to their offices within minutes. I showed them the old pictures, lent James a copy of Dad's book, *Tasman Trespasser,* and left the meeting knowing they were interested and supportive. Within a few weeks they had deposited the money into my bank account.

It wasn't enough to buy a boat, but it was just the injection of enthusiasm and confidence I needed and now I could tell other sponsorship prospects I had someone on board. This was always a tricky question, and one I'd needed to sidestep up to now. It was great when I was next asked who else was involved, not to have to say, 'At this stage, no one.'

It would be another three months before I had another positive response. By this time I had contacted over 290 different companies, posting each a separate proposal, the vast majority of whom I would never hear back from. At breaking point and feeling as if there was no one else to turn to, I decided to approach a new sport radio programme, Radio Live Sport.

Most other radio stations had turned me away when I had offered an interview, but Scott Walker from Live Sport asked me to come into his office for a chat. The meeting went well and we discussed possible media opportunities in the near future and he said he'd see if TV3 would also be interested in covering the story. Slowly my media coverage was building. Finally, I was developing a campaign and event that could deliver sponsors some very good value in terms of coverage, which was now guaranteed in *New Zealand Geographic* and on Radio Live Sport.

The best thing happened just after that meeting.

I was talking with an old friend who worked in the same building, within earshot of a radio show host, Jono Pryor, from

The Rock FM, one of the largest radio stations in New Zealand. I was telling him about how my other friend, Cameron Pocock, had said in a drunken moment of folly, 'If Quincey rows the Tasman I'll cut off my right nut with a rusty machete.' Jono overheard this and asked if he could have my friend's phone number to call him on air that afternoon and ask him about what he'd promised. I was a little hesitant about the reaction he might get but I was at the stage where I really didn't care and was hoping it might generate some sponsorship interest.

The phone call was made and Cameron, to his credit, did a great job in letting people know what I was trying to do as well as telling New Zealand that if I made it then he would be removing his left nut. As horrific as this act might be, it certainly created a following and every couple of weeks The Rock would ring me or Cameron for updates on my progress. This in turn provided a consistent following of supporters and no doubt some people who probably wanted to see Cam go under the knife.

A few weeks after that I took a phone call from Mark Jennings at TV3, saying that Scott Walker from Radio Live Sport had been in touch. TV3 was interested in covering the story and offering some sponsorship. I took this call just after I had been issued with my second lack of warrant of fitness fine in one day, which was going to cost me a total of $400 and was busy arguing with the traffic warden who had issued me with both of them.

Thankfully, I had calmed down a bit and answered the phone appropriately. I don't think I have ever been so angry and bitter only to have my world suddenly turned around, with just one phone call. I was completely full of beans and couldn't care less about my fines now. I had three fantastic media outlets — print, radio and television — all following my expedition and felt as though I finally had the complete tool set to approach sponsors with a new sense of enthusiasm.

As well as covering the story themselves, TV3 agreed to supply other sponsors with a certain amount of advertising time if they agreed to sponsor me with cash. Empowered with being able to offer sponsors mainstream advertising as well as space on the boat and radio coverage, I couldn't wait to get on the phone and start calling around and letting the corporate world know.

A full day on the phone later and still no one was interested. Yet again I'd set my expectations too high and was deeply disappointed with the corporate world. I made 48 unsuccessful calls that day. While all of them asked for proposals I only had 12 left and wasn't willing to part with a single one unless they were willing to meet me to discuss sponsorship.

Frustration was the theme of my life. I'd now been working on the campaign for eight months and while I'd been helped out with some cool products and the incredibly useful loan of a van from Eagle & Franich Construction, the only direct financial support I'd received was the grand total of $2000.

It was late June and Lisa had gone to Fiji for a week with her flatmate. I was starting to have some major doubts about my ability to pull the campaign together. The fear of failure began to build, a little more each day. I couldn't imagine pulling out of the campaign but it was looking so unrealistic. I still wanted to leave Australia in early November, but I don't think anyone around me thought I was being realistic.

I was determined I was going to make it, but sometimes even I wondered why I kept trying. Failure really wasn't an option and I didn't want to even consider not sharing the accolades with my father. The thought of one day watching someone else claim the first west–east solo crossing just wasn't on, so I continued to get on the phone and attempt to sell my cause.

In late June *New Zealand Geographic* ran a one-page story about what I was trying to achieve and a few days later I received an email. It was from Peter Buckley, at Timex Watches New Zealand. From out of the blue his email said Timex would like to know some more about how they could be involved and what sort of support I was after.

Another springboard to the Quincey peak of enthusiasm. This was fantastic, although by now I'd learned to temper my wild optimism, so I was slightly hesitant as I arranged a meeting, knowing all too well these offers can disappear as fast as they arrive. We made a time and I set off to meet Peter and the Timex team.

Arriving at their head office, I jumped into the lift slightly sweaty with nerves, wondering if this meeting would bring me a step closer towards my goal or would I be coming down in the lift a step further away?

I was introduced to Peter, the General Manager, and Vanessa, the Marketing Manager, and was soon telling them about Dad's story and where I needed help. While the meeting ended with no obvious result, we all got on well and shared a few laughs about why on earth I wanted to row the Tasman.

I left the meeting feeling positive but on edge, wondering if they would sponsor me. A week went by, then I emailed Peter to ask whether they would come on board. He told me they were interested but would like to discuss a few more ideas and could we organize another meeting. That sounded promising, but in the back of my head was the fact that with each day they took to make the decision, my departure was being delayed. When I arrived at Timex Peter asked if there had been any developments with any other sponsors, but I had nothing to report.

He then proceeded to tell me they had been checking my proposal over the past week and it had received the legal tick of approval. They would like to make an offer to become my first major financial sponsor.

Woooohoooo! Bursting with excitement I struggled to contain myself. After eight and a half months I finally had a major sponsor, who truly believed in the adventure and my ability to complete the mission. Peter and Vanessa were a wonderful team to have on board — Timex had a heap of great watches and they would be integral as the campaign developed. The injection of cash from Timex meant I could finally buy the boat. I sped home and immediately ordered the kit and designs from London and was told the boat would arrive in three weeks!

A major box was ticked and I was moving in the right direction after being stagnant for some time. The only problem with the Timex sponsorship was that within three hours of receiving it I'd already spent 95 per cent. I urgently needed to find a source of significant cash flow to fund building *TTII* and maintain the momentum, so with *TTII* on her way from London I borrowed $12,000 by using the yet-to be-built boat as security. This would be enough to keep me moving forward.

The Timex sponsorship gave me an excuse to celebrate and I decided to organize my first big fund-raising party. I held it at the Masonic Tavern in Devonport, a pub I'd grown up in over the years. The party was a great excuse to invite everyone who had helped me over the past eight months and also provided a social forum to give everyone an update on what was going on and announce the Timex sponsorship.

Before the party I had felt very alone, and that none of my mates had really taken much interest; in some cases I thought they'd written me off as someone chasing an impossible dream. This certainly wasn't the case, and I had no trouble filling the pub with old and new mates, plus a collection of supporters I didn't know I had. I was humbled by the amount of support and we raised a good sum of money to keep things moving along.

With the Timex deal in place I contacted TV3 to let them know and received no reply. I waited a week before sending another email and then waited another week. I decided a phone call was needed and was met with a few different answer phones and left messages accordingly, slightly panicked as I had promised Timex TV coverage. I had no idea what to do or how to handle the situation. My nightmare scenario was a phone call to Timex telling them I could no longer guarantee TV coverage.

An entire month went by and still I heard nothing.

Finally, I woke up at Lisa's house one morning feeling extremely pissed off about not hearing anything and that this was putting my expedition in jeopardy. I discussed this with Lisa, who agreed. I decided to make a personal appearance at TV3, with my rowing machine, and I wouldn't stop rowing until someone spoke to me.

I called Tony Reid, a reporter at TV3 who had been great to communicate with, and told him I was going to turn up with my rowing machine in about 10 minutes. I knew very well this was a slightly risky manoeuvre and could result in no coverage

77

at all, but I had started to develop a new level of drive and commitment to my sponsors, and I needed some answers.

I arrived at TV3, half expecting to be told to leave. Tony had clearly made it known how determined I was and I was greeted by the PA for the head of the news department. I responded cautiously, only to be offered a meeting with the Head of News at 10.30 a.m., which was two hours away. With the rowing machine poised and ready in the van I decided it wasn't needed and waited patiently for the meeting, which went very well. I left with a commitment from TV3 and was able to honour my commitment with Timex.

The hunt for sponsorship never ceased and probably accounted for 80 per cent of the workload determining my success or failure. Product sponsorship slowly reduced the gaps in my budget as key items were found, while financial sponsorship was the putty that filled those final gaps and covered costs that had to be met with cold hard cash. Ultimately, this was my greatest challenge and the time it took away from building the boat and training certainly limited my life outside the campaign, with every dollar funnelled towards *TTII*.

As *TTII* was being built I was constantly on the phone — project-managing the build and trying to manage finances, as well as media and current sponsors. I hit the wall in the middle of September and with no other sponsors coming on board I had to put everything on hold while I planned my next step.

At this stage the list of companies contacted had grown to 390, and I had made a list, recording their various responses. I started calling every single one to give them an update and try to regenerate some interest.

Eventually, I came across Orcon Internet, who according to my earlier notes were very enthusiastic about the idea but didn't think it could work for them, which sounded to me as though it was worth another crack. I posted my updated proposal to Orcon and followed up with a phone call to some people I knew in the organization, to get some insight into the inner workings of Orcon and an idea of what my chances might be. To my surprise they were interested.

This time I mentally prepared myself for a campaign-changing meeting, readying myself for both the best and the worst possible result. The meeting went well but annoyingly didn't finish with a conclusive decision and I would spend the next few weeks in limbo, wondering whether it was 'deal or no deal'. In the end, I received a call from a guy in charge of purchasing media space for Orcon, asking if they would be able to get some time on TV3. Thankfully, I had the TV3 agreement in place and Orcon came on board as my second major financial sponsor.

Once again I was full of energy and now more than ever I felt sure of getting to Australia. After 390 noes I had finally found another yes, which made every single one of those rejections seem worthwhile.

The hunt for sponsorship would continue through the entire campaign and even when I was on the water, I had many great mates and supporters who purchased their names on the boat for $50 and I was extremely grateful for every single one, as I certainly needed to rely on those smaller donations from time to time.

Dad had always said to me that 90 per cent of the battle was getting to the start line and now I knew exactly what he meant. While I eventually left Australia with a sense of achievement at making it so far, I knew I owed the opportunity to fulfil my dream and prove myself against the Tasman to so many other people; some of them had loaned me money I still needed to repay, and all had put faith in me when I needed it most. I was determined not to let any of them down. I also knew I could never put a price on the feeling that would come with finally achieving my goal if I made it all the way across to New Zealand.

9　A boat in bits

The day had come and my boat had arrived, much later than I had hoped, but she was here and that was all that mattered. The process of importing her was far more of a rigmarole than I ever anticipated, and the fact that I'd parted with over $13,500 was never far from my mind as I waited for her to arrive.

The flat pack of plywood didn't quite take a straight route from Heathrow to Auckland in a couple of days, as I had naively expected. Instead the trip would take a laborious three weeks. I had forked out an extra $1000 to have the kitset flown out from the UK rather than wait around two months for it to creep its way over by ship. In a strange way I kind of wanted to be the first person to take *TTII* on the water.

By the time *TTII* arrived she had been on a worldwide expedition, spending a week on the tarmac at Heathrow because apparently no one knew where she was going. Expecting her to have landed in Auckland I had rounded up a few mates to help me start building the weekend she was expected.

I called Customs at Auckland International Airport only to be told my consignment hadn't left the UK. When I tracked down the freight company I was told this was the normal process, and that *TTII* was on a wait list. I would just have to be patient. I waited another week and again organized some mates, only to be told by the UK freight company that my boat was now on the tarmac in Abu Dhabi. This probably seems fairly standard to a freight forwarder or someone in the industry, but to me it sounded crazy and was incredibly frustrating. I was eventually told I needed to wait until there was room on a plane to slip in my 33 flat pieces of plywood.

My plywood finally arrived in New Zealand and once again impatience was probably my worst enemy as I argued with Customs as to why they needed to keep treated timber over the weekend. All I wanted was to be able to start building my boat but someone decided my boat was a threat to bio-security and I had to wait for them to stamp a bit of paper.

At around this point in time I got a phone call from Express Logistics in Auckland, who earlier on had agreed to export my boat for free from New Zealand to Australia, once it had been built. I told the guys what had been going on and they immediately swung into action. With a few phone calls the boat was ready to be released the next day.

Importing the boat really highlighted one of my major weaknesses, and one I needed to work on — my complete lack of interest in systems involving paperwork and reading the smaller details. I guess I struggle to understand why we need so many systems and I'm a bit too trusting about people doing an effective job.

I was ready by the phone at 8 a.m. waiting for the call to say I could go and pick her up from the airport. By 9 a.m. the beautiful call arrived, directing me to a particular warehouse in South Auckland where she would be waiting. After effusively thanking the guy on the end of the phone I was in my building clothes and into the Eagle & Franich van.

Driving to the airport seemed to take forever and of course every single traffic light was red, giving me plenty of time to call Salthouse Boatbuilders, telling them I would start building that afternoon.

First stop was the freight forwarder, Express Logistics, to collect the paperwork confirming *TTII* wasn't carrying any infectious diseases, and they directed me around the corner to pick her up. When I got there, three blokes were having a smoke in a small shed outside a large warehouse. I handed the papers over and said I was looking for 33 sheets of plywood with shapes cut out of the sheets, not knowing how the parcel was packaged or what sort of condition it was in. I waited by the front door as one of the workers sped off on a fork lift. The fork lift appeared back around the corner with a big wobbly stack of chipped and damaged plywood that had clearly seen better days, with large chunks out of the side.

Somehow I needed to squeeze this 400 kg pack of plywood into the van and get it to Salthouse Boatbuilders. I asked the guy on the forklift if he thought it was going to fit in the van — and rather than answering me directly, the challenge was on. He slid the pack into the back, at one stage lifting the van off the ground as he manoeuvred the pack around.

Finally squeezed into the van, *TTII* and I started our first trip together from South to North Auckland, arriving at Salthouse Boatbuilders at around 1 p.m. My first job was unloading each sheet from the van into the shed where I would spend the next three months. John Salthouse, the founding boat builder, told me my Dad's boat was built about 8 m away from where I was about to start. I thought that was fairly unique and felt privileged to be building my boat here, where there was so much history.

Once I'd unloaded the ply I asked myself the inevitable question. How on earth do I build a boat? I didn't have the faintest idea, so I began reading the manual and started chopping out the odd piece of plywood and stacking the various pieces into piles, hoping I was doing the right thing. Revelling in what I felt was my first tangible step towards rowing the Tasman, I stayed at Salthouse until about 9 p.m., reluctant to head home.

I couldn't wait to see her start to take shape and arrived back early the next day, ready to start sticking *TTII* together. My good mate Richard Vaughan came down to help and we worked like madmen, cutting out all the shapes and sanding the edges, preparing to stick the different parts together, neither of us really knowing quite what was going on. Richard eventually had to leave and I started to try to put *TTII* together, slowly finding what looked like the right part and fumbling my way through the plans and cryptic instructions.

I managed to get the basic hull frames and supporting stringers in place before I started to lose confidence in what I was doing. The guys at Salthouse had suggested a few people who would be available to help me build *TTII* and while I had initially wanted to build her myself it was proving both time consuming and challenging.

Chris Salthouse (Curly) introduced me to a boat builder by the name of Dave Yallop, who was looking for work. He'd worked at Salthouse before and Curly assured me Dave would be a good man to have on board. He agreed to start work in a few days, by which time I'd asked the guys about some basic boat-building skills I might need to know so I wouldn't make a complete fool of myself in front of Dave.

Dave arrived before me at 7.30 a.m. and had already brought in all his tools and equipment and was reading over the plans. After we sat down and discussed a bit of a game plan, he inspected some of my handiwork with a cheeky smile. We decided it was best if we started again. I needed to use some of Dave's tools and he peered over as I rummaged through his kit and picked out what I thought would do the job. If I used a particular tool the wrong way Dave abruptly told me off, removed the weapon and replaced it with the correct tool.

After feeling as if I was back in woodwork class at school, I became Dave Yallop's unofficial apprentice, in an interesting relationship where I was the boss in a monetary sense but Dave was leading the way in building the boat. As the weeks went past and I slowly reduced the number of mistakes I was making, the amount of time Dave spent on the boat was limited by the money I had coming in the door and whether I could afford to pay him or not.

Being a good man, if I couldn't pay him he would either leave me with clear instructions on how to continue or keep working, telling me to pay him when I could. I was very lucky to have landed a great builder like Dave, and very lucky to be surrounded by a collection of boat builders and engineers whose combined skills meant that to complete most jobs I only had to walk across the yard to get advice or build something for the boat. It was very important for me to have the expertise of the other boat builders around as a lot of the time they forced me to slow my thinking down. They made sure I built and designed attachments completely correctly, knowing the pressure some of the attachments would be under once I was out on the Tasman.

The two metalwork engineers, Pete and Kane, who helped me

construct my rowlocks, sliding seat rails and foot block were fantastic at talking me through the process of what we were trying to build. They were absolutely essential and I couldn't have asked for two better or more skilled blokes to work with. When you're rushing through a project it's important to have people who force you to slow down a bit and reflect on each decision. Pete and Kane made me do this but also managed to keep the throttle on full bore, which I really appreciated. Sometime they would take the Mickey as well, explaining things slowly, as if I had the IQ of a chocolate chip muffin, which in hindsight was fairly true when it came to working with metal.

TTII would be at Salthouse Boatbuilders for three months before she was ready to go into the water. The boat-building yard was a magical place and certainly a highlight of the entire expedition was being able to spend time down at the yard, putting my boat together right next to where my father's had been built.

10 The million-metre row

To prepare for the Tasman I knew that as well as building a boat, I also needed to put myself through an incredibly intense and challenging physical test. I needed to know how my body would hold up in an extreme endurance environment and, more importantly, how my mind would hold up. I had a few thoughts around what I could possibly do as a test for the Tasman, such as a 10-day tramp with a oversized pack or I could have cycled from Auckland to Wellington, but I wanted to have a go at some sort of record.

An idea popped into my head when I was reading about two guys preparing for an Atlantic rowing crossing as a pair, who attempted to break the world record for rowing a million metres together. I'd never heard of any such record before, so I went on to the Internet. The official world record for a single million-metre row was 128 hours, 38 minutes and 19.0 seconds, set a few years earlier by an Englishman, Nigel Gower.

As soon as I read that I knew I wanted to give it a crack.

By this stage *Tasman Trespasser II* was almost ready to go into the water. Her frame was finished and all we needed was paint and some rowlocks. While finishing the boat was my number one priority, at the same time as all the building work had been going on, I was also planning a separate campaign to try to break the million-metre (1000 km) indoor rowing world record.

Although I didn't have any money to pay for everything I would need, thankfully Horley's Supplements New Zealand sponsored some food and made it possible. I thought it would provide a great fund-raising opportunity, and hopefully some publicity, leading in turn to more sponsorship.

I'd been working on the boat frantically over the last month and had left my preparation for the world record attempt to the last minute. The real purpose of the record attempt was to test myself — I needed to push myself to the very limit of tiredness and sleep deprivation to figure out what started to get sore and also to see how my epilepsy reacted to extreme fatigue.

I had tried to train for this event with a combination of weight training and endurance rowing-machine sessions of up to nine hours at a time. At this stage my biggest rowing effort would have been around 145 km in one sitting, so a huge aspect of the million-metres would be a mental test, and I had no idea how to prepare for that part. Initially, I thought the event could be run in a radio station, which would have provided great publicity, but there were problems with 24-hour security and support-crew access so I decided to run it at my surf club, Mairangi Bay.

The surf club would provide a great environment. I'd be able to have my friends and support crew around me and whoever wanted to stay through the night would be able to, as I spent 17 glorious hours a day on the bloody machine. The week before was hectic as usual, meeting sponsor prospects, building the boat and arranging media for the million-metre event. As I became more and more swamped with things, all of which had to be done, I started to realize I needed to start forming the team which would end up helping me get across the Tasman.

I already had Olly, who was awesome but he was also busy with his own work and commitments. A few people approached asking whether they could help in some way, all of which I appreciated, but I needed to be sure they had the skills to control me when I was losing the plot — both in the million-metre challenge and while I was in the middle of the Tasman. Along with being a huge challenge and testing period for me, this attempt would also be a selection process for who I wanted to act as my official land manager while I was crossing the ditch.

I called a meeting of all my mates I thought might be interested in helping out, many of them highly skilled surf lifeguards and athletes. I'd written a list outlining what exactly I needed help with and where exactly they might be able to contribute. After about an hour we'd created a roster of who would be next to me at all times to ensure I was never alone while I was rowing, as being constantly supervised was part of the criteria for the Guinness World Record Association. This was fantastic and would provide a great structure for me to be constantly entertained with new people and hopefully distracted by a variety of mates.

When I got home I noticed a good friend, Michael Buck, had volunteered to sit with me every night except one, and most days. Michael had shown a huge commitment; he was also in the national surf-lifesaving team and was currently a world record holder in his own right in beach relay, and as part of the 4x50 metre obstacle race team. Having someone of his level of sporting experience on my side was huge and I was very happy to have him around. Another of Michael's great attributes was his ability to deal with media, and having competed as a New

Zealand rep he knew about pressure. The more I thought about it in the lead-up to the million-metre challenge, the more I wanted Michael to be a part of my adventure. Not only was he a great mate but his combination of skills was unmatched, and it was going to be interesting to see how he dealt with me as I attempted to row 1000 km.

It was Tuesday, the day before the million-metres. Dave the boat builder and I were fibreglassing the inside of the cabin, a solid two-man job with me inside the cabin getting covered in resin and breathing in some solid fumes. The boat took up most of the day but I was happy because that completed the last of the complicated building and I would come back to a nearly completed *TTII*.

The basic plan was to row for 17 hours a day for the next five days, with short breaks throughout for a combination of sleeping and eating. I would have to hold a certain pace over those 17 hours and aim to row 200 km per day. If I managed to do this for five days I would break the world record by five hours.

By 6 p.m. I'd collected most of the equipment: sponsors' banners, five days' worth of food, mattresses and of course the Concept 2 rowing machine. The Surf Club needed to be set up for a 7 a.m. rowing start in the morning. A couple of people showed up to help set up and by 10.30 that night the room looked great. The food was ready, the room was ready, we had a TV crew showing up in the morning and everything had fallen into place. A few friends were still around and we shared some last-minute jokes about how my backside would never forgive me for what was about to happen.

When they all left I tried to get to sleep on the floor next to the rowing machine. Although I was very tired after a hectic week, in reality I was overtired, overexcited and I'd probably had the worst preparation I could possibly have for this event. When I looked at the clock it was midnight and it was around 1 a.m. before I eventually got to sleep.

A knock on the door at 5.45 a.m. from the TV3 crew wanting to set up for the breakfast news woke me; I let them in before climbing back into bed to hopefully catch some more sleep.

Michael arrived at around 7 a.m., after his swimming training, and the other surf lifeguards and supporters started to flow in. I'd had breakfast about an hour before and had lined up my five drink bottles for the day. I'd also polished the sliding rail, which the Concept 2 rower relied upon. With 20 minutes to go I went to the bathroom and added a few coats of anti-chafing cream as well as dealing with my last-minute nerves.

Friends and family surrounded me and two cameramen stood within a few feet, ready to broadcast live on national TV. With every minute planned on a complicated spreadsheet showing exactly how I was going to row the million-metres, with one minute to go I was asked to do an interview on the TV3 breakfast show, which delayed the start by 15 minutes. The timing was unfortunate, but I was well aware of the benefit of TV time, so happily obliged.

Back on the rowing seat everybody began a 10-second countdown and before I knew it I was on my way, with no idea how my body was going to cope. I smiled away, not really having much else to worry about as I watched the metres roll past. The first 80 km were very relaxing and I was comfortable knowing I only needed to be where I was right now, and there was nothing else I needed to be doing.

By about 90 km, after close to eight hours of rowing, my

backside started to hurt like it had never done before, and I sent Michael on his first task — to find a backside cushion. Michael arrived back with a square 15 cm thick piece of foam, which covered the entire seat. At first I was doubtful, thinking it was too big, but as soon as I started rowing, I knew Michael has found the world's best rowing seat, as it almost instantly dissolved the pressure pain I had been developing.

My next biggest challenge was eating the volume of food I needed in the short 15 minute breaks I had allowed myself, and then keeping it down long enough for my body to process. As I was constantly vomiting small amounts of food, it was incredibly challenging. While my first day had started late I made up a little bit of time and at this stage we were ahead of schedule, with 200 km rowed. At midnight I decided to get some sleep, happy that I'd achieved my target for the first day.

The next day I woke up slightly sore and a little weak, but still felt strong enough to get on and row another 200 km. The morning went well and we were on track, hitting all the targets. I'd become a little better at keeping food down and Michael was slightly better at convincing me to stick to the schedule with help from my friend Olly, who had showed up. I was slowly chipping away through the kilometres, but by about 10 p.m. that night the distance seemed to tick by ever so slowly.

With only Michael in the room the temptation to pull out started to enter my mind and I squashed it as quickly as I could. By 1 a.m. I had missed the target for the day by 10 km and had to decide whether to stop and get some sleep or carry on. I chose sleep, dreading the next day when I would have to make up the missing kilometres.

Day 3 and I woke up in a world of pain — everything seemed to hurt and even pulling gently on the rower was awful, but I still thought I would reach halfway by lunch time. With that in mind I plowed into the morning. Even by missing my breaks as I tried to get back on target, I didn't reach halfway until about 3 p.m. Rowing 500 km in less than three days was the most I'd ever rowed, but it was only halfway.

I took an hour off rowing, then it was a battle to convince myself to get back on the machine. Eventually, I would row another 40 km that night, taking me twice as long as usual. At 1 p.m. I climbed into bed, promising Michael and Cam I would get up at 3 a.m. to continue rowing. They were staying the night at the club with me and would both make sure I woke up.

The alarm went off at 2.55 a.m. and I woke shivering uncontrollably, so much so I could hardly sit on the machine. Thinking it was the cold, I decided to start rowing and the shivering finally subsided over the next half an hour, conveniently taking my mind away from the fact that it was also my birthday and I would be spending it rowing on an indoor bloody rowing machine.

I knew Lisa would be bringing me some special birthday food, but the way my mind was going I was struggling to maintain my composure as people walked in and out. As the morning ticked over a couple of people watching asked how I was feeling and some even commented on how tired I was looking, almost prompting me to throw my toys out of the cot. Thankfully, Michael picked up on some of this and typed up a small poster for people to read as they came in. While I was very grateful for all the support, I needed to focus intensely if I was going to get anywhere near the world record and the fact that I was so off target and torturing my body diminished my ability to interact.

Lisa finally arrived with my birthday lunch — a stack of

pancakes. They looked absolutely awesome but at the time I was unable to express how great it was to see her and barely even acknowledged she was there.

It was a hard time for both of us — I was battling to get through the next 200 km and Lisa could do nothing to help. By the end of the fourth day I was completely shattered and had just ticked over 700 km. I'd hardly slept and the pressure was coming down on me, with TV and radio stations constantly calling Michael for updates, asking him if he still thought I was capable of completing a million metres.

Day 5 started on time, but after a few hours the left side of my chest started to cramp, feeling as if something was biting the muscles. I told Michael about this and took a few Panadol to relieve the pain, which continued to get worse and tear at my chest. The pain increased until I stopped rowing to allow a physiotherapist to take a look. She massaged my chest gently, relieving the pain a bit, and I suggested putting a seatbelt around my chest as a form of compression bandage, which seemed to relieve the problem, though only for a short while.

Somehow I managed to slog out a further 50 km but by then the pain was intense. Michael called a paramedic friend, concerned with the level of pain coming from my chest and worried that I could be experiencing a heart attack.

After sitting completely still for close to two hours the pain reduced slightly, enough to let me climb back on the rower. I could hardly pull the handle towards myself and I rowed the next 50 km with straight arms, to see if I could get through enough kilometres to make a mark on the record. By 5 p.m. it was obvious the record was out of reach. I couldn't row properly and with my chest in pain I withdrew from the record attempt at 802 km, rowed over five days.

It took me a while to summon up the courage to call Lisa and tell her I'd pulled the pin and wanted a ride home. I also found it very hard to tell Michael and my friend Cam that I'd had enough and was giving up, after they'd both stuck it out with me over the whole five days. I turned my cell phone off and waited for Lisa to arrive and take me back home. While I waited the odd supporter showing up and I had to tell them the news.

When I got home I couldn't sleep, due no doubt to a combination of chest pain and disappointment. At 6 p.m. I turned on my phone to find I'd missed 26 calls and within a few moments I was on the radio explaining to a collection of radio hosts how I'd given up and wouldn't be continuing. While it was hugely disappointing on one level, in my own head I knew that while I hadn't made the million-metre mark, I'd passed my own personal test, with not a single sign of my epilepsy.

Over the five days I rowed I had over 200 visitors, some of whom donated to the cause by paying $50 to have their name on my boat. This raised a small amount of money, which I used to pay Dave while I stayed at home and hit the phones for more sponsorship.

I saw the challenge as a small success and happily shrugged off the seeds of doubt the odd person tried to plant about not being ready for the Tasman if I couldn't row 1000 km. What was great about the whole thing was that Michael had gained a huge amount of experience dealing with the media and had proved himself to be an incredible support when I was exhausted. I now knew he'd make a fantastic land support manager, another success I was able to take from what other people might see as a failure.

After all, I'd faced a massive physical challenge with no epilepsy and gained valuable media attention, which my current sponsors loved, and hopefully I would be able to turn that exposure into some more sponsorship opportunities.

Another advantage of finishing the challenge early was that I was now able to get down to *TTII* the next day and get back into preparing her for the Tasman. Time was running out and I needed to put all my effort into getting *TTII* into the water and tested.

11 *TTII* is in the water

I woke up with a moderate pain in my lower abdomen. I put it down to my exercise and weights routine over the past week, thinking it was probably a minor strain. Lisa had headed off to work and the plan was to send a few more sponsorship emails, then head down to the boat. She was in the final stages and any day now I would be putting her in the water.

All I could think about was getting *TTII* wet and taking her for the first row up and down the Greenhithe River, just as Dad had done 35 years ago. The moment was so very close and I was pushing hard, spending some fairly late nights down at the boat and mornings trying to raise more funds to keep the project moving.

By 9 a.m. I'd made a few calls and sent a few emails. The small pain in my lower abdomen started to increase into a more crippling, deep-set pain. I went through my usual routine when I start to feel sick — going to the bathroom and trying to vomit, as that sometimes clears a blockage, but this just seemed to aggravate the pain levels and left me sitting on the bathroom floor wondering what on earth was happening in my gut.

I dragged myself off the bathroom floor, into the Eagle & Franich van and up the road to the local Accident and Emergency Centre. I had a slightly uncomfortable drive, helped with a few painkillers, and arrived at the doctor's surgery complaining of a sore lower abdomen. The nurse asked me if I'd eaten anything strange over the past 24 hours — I'd had some Thai takeaways but this wasn't unusual and I'd never had any trouble with their food before. The nurse then asked if I'd had my appendix removed. I knew no one had taken it out, but this was something that had never even occurred to me.

The doctor asked a few questions, then told me to lie back while he pushed down on the tender part of my lower abdomen. As he released the pressure of his hand from my stomach this immediately sent a sharp and excruciating pain through my body. I let rip a few expletives before apologizing and clutching my stomach.

The doctor then asked if I had anything important on over the next few weeks, as he was about to book me in for surgery that afternoon to remove my appendix. A number of thoughts popped into my head, the main one being how this was going to reduce the time I had to test *TTII* before we left for Australia.

He offered to call an ambulance but I wanted to get home to collect my laptop and a few sponsorship proposals to work on while I was trapped in a hospital bed, unsure what surgery would involve and how long it would take. On the drive home I called Lisa and told her I was off to hospital.

We'd made some plans for the weekend, so we were both disappointed, but she was at my bedside within a few hours of me arriving at Auckland Hospital, with some magazines and her smiling, supportive face. I arrived at lunch time and was loaded up with painkillers by 1 p.m. and booked in for surgery that evening. I guess I could have taken the fact that I was going to be seriously slowed down over the next few weeks fairly badly, and I could have focused on how it was going to slow down almost every aspect of my preparation. Instead I chose to start researching recovery times and methods of faster recovery from an appendectomy to help me get back down to the boat ASAP and get on with training. The appendix had to go, there was nothing I could do about it; just as well this hadn't happened in the middle of the Tasman. It was way better to stay positive and find solutions than kick up a fuss.

The operation went well, the surgeons using keyhole surgery to remove my inflamed appendix, pulling the sucker out of my bellybutton and leaving only a few small scars. I woke in the morning a little tired and tender, determined to get on with recovering. The first step would be getting out of the hospital bed to head downstairs and across the road to a coffee shop for a muffin and a flat white.

I ended up in the same queue as the surgeon who had removed my appendix. As this was just before morning rounds, I asked if he would pop in and discharge me first as I was feeling good enough to get home. The surgeon made it in to see me, checked me out and as a result I was diagnosed, admitted, operated on and discharged in under 24 hours.

Then followed a compulsory three days of doing nothing, which was a bit of a pain, but gave me a few days to catch up on communications with a few sponsors and suppliers. After the rest I was back down to the boat, where Dave had made great progress. It was wonderful having someone I could trust working on the boat when I wasn't there, and knowing that progress hadn't stopped had helped put my mind at ease while I'd been laid up.

Recovery from surgery went very well, considering how many times I pushed my luck lifting the odd sheet of plywood and sanding various parts of the boat. After about a week we were back on schedule, with a few mates coming down to the boat shed to help out where they could and Dave continuing to work hard. Although I still had a couple of holes in my stomach, I was back to 90 per cent after around 10 days. I gingerly climbed back on a rowing machine to see what sort of effect the general anaesthetic had had on me, managing to row around 10 km.

Two weeks after the surgery Friday came along and I took a call from the shipping company, letting me know that the last opportunity for me to ship the boat to Australia would be in five weeks. If I missed it I would have to wait another month. Once again the pressure was on and I needed to finish *TTII* and get her trialled and tested before she disappeared for a month, on her first crossing of the Tasman.

Frantically working on the boat now, I had to be careful not to strain too much to avoid reopening my stomach stitches. Somehow I made time to organize a surprise night out with Lisa, involving a ferry ride to Waiheke Island for dinner, to say thanks for the extra effort of looking after me in hospital and putting up with a crook boyfriend. I also knew that from that point on I would be focused entirely on the expedition, and because I wanted her to still be there when it was all over, I knew I had to make sure we were OK.

Friday night was booked in and I'd arranged mates to come and help me get *TTII* ready for launch, with a solid working bee arranged for Saturday and Sunday. Before I could fix my seat on the boat I needed to widen the axle for the wheels which rolled my seat back and forward. This involved separating a piece of metal glued onto a piece of wood. My tool of choice for this procedure would be a freshly sharpened chisel.

I slowly pushed the chisel edge under the lip of the piece of metal and pushed as hard as I could, not paying attention to the fact that my other hand was holding the wood down. The chisel suddenly popped the metal off the wood and glided straight into my hand, digging into the top of my thumb and filleting the inside of my palm. It left a 10 cm gash, exposing my thumb bone and leaving me numb with shock as I looked down to see my hand completely opened up.

The very first reaction I had was to check the function of the thumb, my greatest concern being that I had sliced through tendons and ligaments essential to my hand being able to control an oar. Thankfully, I'd missed most of them and I could freely move my thumb around and even see how the bone moved inside my hand. This provided a slight level of relief as I hoped it just meant a bucketload of stitches.

I slid the chisel out of my hand, revealing the extent of the damage and of course the gash immediately started to bleed all over the floor and my shorts. By now I was feeling a bit light-headed and called Dave over to help, showing him the hole in my hand and the pool of blood.

Dave's eyes widened and he grabbed rag covered with acetone and sawdust. We both looked at it and thought perhaps it was worth getting a clean one. I stepped outside and sat down, as I thought fainting could be on the cards as I went into shock. Dave passed me a cleaner rag and I wrapped up my hand. He offered to drive me to hospital and I think he was disappointed when I said I wanted him to keep working on the boat and I would sort it out.

I took a few moments outside to suck in a few deep breaths before walking up to the office to arrange a ride. I took it very slowly. The office was about 300 m away and I left a trail of blood behind me as I walked up the stairs. I made it to the top then had to sit and ask for help.

When the office staff came out I showed them the cut and asked if someone could drop me up the road to the local doctor's surgery. When they saw the cut they sprang into action and I was whipped up the road, only to be told at the surgery that I needed to go to Middlemore Hospital, on the other side of Auckland. Fortunately for me, the Salthouse Boatbuilders' accountant happily offered to take me, rather than waiting for an ambulance. Damn — another weekend in hospital with Lisa giving up her free time to come and hang out with me. Worst of all, I'd have to tell her about Waiheke and ask her to cancel her own surprise date.

The next three days would be slightly different from my earlier 24-hour hospital experience. I arrived at Middlemore and began what would end up being 50 hours in the waiting room before I was finally seen by a doctor and admitted to surgery. My cut was explored under general anaesthetic and I woke up with 28 stitches and a few days' worth of antibiotics. Yet again I was faced with the decision to either get upset about the situation or to move on and look for solutions to stay on track.

I was at the hospital from Friday till Sunday afternoon, so there wasn't really any progress to look forward to seeing on Monday, but I still needed to get down there as early as I could to keep things on track, even with only one working hand making for slow progress.

My injured hand was wrapped up in a pile of bandages and covered in plastic bags to make sure none of the dust could work its way into the cut and infect the wound. The cut certainly slowed me down and left an impressive-looking scar, but the greatest effect was on my physical training. Within a period of two weeks I'd had two general anaesthetics and only one 10 km row, with three and possibly four weeks of inactivity ahead of me while my hand healed — enough to set back the fitness base I'd developed by now.

After about six days of limited progress on *TTII* I removed the stitches at home. The cut had healed remarkably well and with no time to waste I jumped on the indoor rower and made sure I could still row. Thankfully, it all held together and I was back on track. The cut in my hand frightened me a bit and really made me slow down and reflect on how fragile we humans actually are — after all, if something similar happened on the Tasman, the trip would be over. It was a sobering thought.

The next two weeks were full on, with every day down at the boat to get it ready for launch day, and fully tested, as well as organizing the signwriting. This was bloody exciting and great fun. Sure it was a large amount of stress, but the people around me were aware of the pressure and ready to increase the level of help they gave, with plenty of days working into the night, sometimes alone or sometimes with others.

TTII was so close to being finished. I had overcome two surgeries and I was on the construction home straight. I arrived at Salthouse Boatbuilders early on a Thursday morning, after spending the previous night working on her knowing that today was the day she would be going in the water.

I was slightly hesitant to rush the work and get her wet, as I knew once she was out of the workshop it would be a hassle to get her back in, but I literally had no choice. With the impending deadline for shipping I needed to test, signwrite, officially launch and fit out the electronics within three weeks, so getting her in the water was a priority. I gathered about nine blokes from around the yard to help me lift *TTII* up onto the trailer inside the shed, so we could roll her down to the water's edge.

I had hurried all morning to get *TTII* ready by lunch time, knowing I'd be pushing to get her in the water. Whatever happened she was going to get wet today, and was on the trailer and almost ready to roll. There was no steering yet, as the rudder system hadn't been sorted out, and my special rowing shoes, which would enable me to steer using my right foot, still hadn't arrived. Too bad. She was going in the water today.

I kept going on the boat till 1.30 that afternoon, fixing as much as I could until it was close to high tide, when all the Salthouse boys would be starting smoko and could give me a hand to get *TTII* into the tide.

Sure enough, nothing would be easy and someone had put a two-ton boat engine between *TTII* and the door to freedom. After convincing one of the guys to move the engine with a forklift and putting up with a barrage of jokes about *TTII* actually needing the engine and that was why it had been put there, it was finally shifted and I started to push *TTII* out the door.

It wasn't easy moving the trailer over a few bumps, so I asked for a bit of help from some of the guys and we clipped *TTII* onto the Eagle & Franich van to reverse her into the water. I gave her one quick blast with the compressed air hose to remove four months of sawdust and she was ready to go. No electrics, no signage, no steering — just me and *TTII*. I manoeuvred around the boat yard and positioned her on the ramp then pulled the hand brake up and hopped out to take a few photos of a long-awaited and important moment.

I looked around and all the Salthouse blokes had stopped work and come out to watch. With the huge respect I had developed for all of the guys this made the moment special, and I was glad to share it with them. One of the guys jumped into my van and told me to hop in *TTII* while he reversed down the ramp.

In she went and the moment was finally here, after 12 months of work and about 10 years of dreaming. I guess I expected to be hit in the face with a barrage of emotion, and I was surprised at my reaction to seeing her go in.

I thought I would be ecstatic and immensely proud, but this wasn't the case. As special as it should have been, there was no way I could savour the moment. While rushing the boat from the shed into the water was a great way to get a few things done, as soon as she hit the water I knew this was the beginning of a new phase which would need more cash and more work. While deep down I still had no idea about how this would all play out, nonetheless it was satisfying to see that she floated.

I took a few moments rowing up and down the river and getting a feel for how she glided through the water and reacted to my touch. Just like a new car, the temptation was there to push the accelerator to the floor and see how she responded, so I threw around a few power strokes. I loved the feel of my new Concept 2 oars as they pushed *TTII* through the water. I'd told Michael about putting her in today, as he was the only one I wanted to be there. We went out for a row up and down the river and he had a few strokes. I'd mentioned the possibility of launching *TTII* to Lisa but she of all people knew how *TTII* stuff changed every minute.

Lisa had become very strategic about asking how things went because I hated talking about it if I hadn't achieved something I'd aimed for, but that day I went home and raved about how great *TTII* was in the water and had a few extra beers to celebrate.

On one occasion I had a spare two hours with the boat so I decided to take her down to Takapuna Beach and see how easy she was going to be to flip. Another problem was that launching *TTII* was no easy task, in fact it was a bit of an ordeal, and I would always find myself recruiting bystanders to roll up their shorts and hold her in the water as I went and parked the van up the road and sprinted back down to the beach.

When I'd done all of that on this occasion, I jumped in *TTII* and rowed out to the middle of the bay and pulled in the oars. The water was very still and smooth enough for me to stand on the side, so I started to rock the boat, not really thinking through the consequences if I did flip and had to drag her back to the beach.

I rocked her up and down as much as I could, trying to get as much of the hull out of the water as possible. I kept trying to do this from different positions in the boat, but she was fairly solid in the water and, for the life of me, I couldn't flip her over.

Each time I took her out for a training row I'd try various other little tests. Altogether I managed to get *TTII* on the water around eight times before shipping her to Australia, but never for more than a couple of hours. So at this stage *TTII* still hadn't been tested overnight, but I had a lot of confidence in her stability.

The next few weeks were hectic to say the least — everything seemed to cost over $1000 and money was running out fast. A key element was coordinating the different people involved, whether it was the electrician, the signwriter or the painters, it was all a case of just doing whatever it took to get the job done and making sure everyone knew about the time constraints.

The days rolled by and gradually jobs were being ticked off the list, the last being installing the electronics. While I had no background in electrics at all, I wanted to be as much a part of the installation process as possible and learn what I could. As it turned out, I was bloody lucky not to have any major electrical issues during the crossing, which was a testament to Bruce, who did a fantastic job on the installation. And I freely admit to having his number programmed into speed dial on the satellite phone!

Even though I'd had an unofficial boat launch with Michael and the Salthouse guys, I knew it was important to invite the media and have an official launch day with all the signwriting completed, to give my sponsors maximum exposure.

It was the night of 8 December and *TTII* needed to be in the container ready to be shipped to Australia in two days' time, so this was my only opportunity to show her off. I'd emailed all my sponsors and friends, asking them to come down to Takapuna Beach to watch Lisa and me try to crack a bottle of champagne over her bow and officially name her *Tasman*

Trespasser II. Eagle & Franich had loaned me a nice big truck for the occasion and after she'd been manoeuvred through a few bollards, *TTII* appeared for a crowd of around 100 supporters and media waiting on the beach.

Timex had erected some flags and I positioned *TTII* between them. Somewhat humbled by the number of people who'd shown up, I felt a small tingle of achievement. For once I had some solid proof to show that I was a serious contender for the Tasman crossing, instead of what had seemed like endless discussion of intangible aspects of the project. A few beers were had that night, and the launch received some coverage on the television news, all contributing to the sponsors feeling valued and getting some great recognition.

With only two days left with *TTII* before she was due to be shipped off to Australia I had to spend a bit more time rowing and both days were filled with small trips around Auckland Harbour and the odd photoshoot.

It was the last night before *TTII* would have to go into the container to be fumigated and shipped to Australia, and with nowhere to put her, I parked *TTII* on the main road outside my flat. Terrified that someone would tamper with her, I peered out my window every hour throughout the night, checking she was safe.

I woke up at around 7 a.m. ready to drive *TTII* out to the freight yard before too much heavy traffic built up. I stopped on the way at a hardware store to purchase a few items I thought I might need, such as strops to secure her in the container and some metal-cutting discs just in case I needed to trim the wheel arches, which were a bit on the wide side. Arriving at the Express Logistics freight yard close to 9 a.m., I was told

I needed to have *TTII* in the container by 11 a.m. when the fumigators would be arriving to decontaminate my boat and the container would be sealed.

Not thinking this would be a problem I was quite relaxed and started to pack the boat with everything I thought I would need in Australia, including all my tools and spare parts. Once *TTII* was loaded I rounded up a few guys to help me roll her in. Lining the wheels up with the door I could see it was going to be tight but we were all sure the trailer would squeeze in. Everyone pushing at ramming speed to get her up and into the container was abruptly jolted forward when both tyres caught on the mouth of the container.

After initially laughing, I took a more calculated approach and measured the axle width and the container door. Oops. The container door was 262 cm wide and the trailer axle was 263 cm. What I had imagined was going to be a satisfying and relatively simple day had just turned into a mad panic.

I dragged out all the tools I'd packed so carefully into the boat, thanking my lucky stars I'd stopped on the way to pick up the metal-cutting discs. I duly attached them to my grinder and my first job was slicing off the wheel arches. Wheel arches removed, the next job was dealing with the lights as they stuck out just as far. I took another measurement as I racked my brain and tried not to lose the plot.

The problem seemed to be the general width of the tyres and so replacing these became the focus of the next 30 minutes. I came up with the idea of using space-saver spare tyres, which are very skinny. I jumped into my van and drove around asking various mechanics if they had any spare space-saver tyres. After trying five different mechanics and secondhand Japanese car part centres, I managed to find one.

The only problem was the trailer was a five-stud setup requiring five holes for the nuts and bolts and the space-saver tyre had four, with none of the holes lining up with the bolts in the trailer.

This being the only possible solution at this stage I took the tyre and headed back to the boat, where the Rentokil guys had arrived to complete their $500 fumigation. There was no way the five bolts on the trailer axle would line up with the holes on the space-saver so I had to cut a new set of holes with my angle grinder, making the tyre completely useless for driving on the road but good enough for a voyage across the Tasman in a container. Space-saver tyre on and wheel arches cut off, it didn't look like much of a trailer.

With help from the Rentokil blokes and the guys from Express Logistics we squeezed *TTII* in, rubber squeaking down each side as the tyres were forced against the container walls. It was now 2 p.m. and after a few high fives and pats on the back the fumigation could begin.

I felt a huge sense of achievement. I'd been working full steam ahead for the past two years to get to this point and I was finally on my way to the start line. This was coupled with a slight sense of relief that I no longer had to spend every spare moment working on the boat. For a month I wouldn't be able to get to her and I could relax for a moment.

The next focus was getting to Sydney, as my money had now officially run out and there were no further signs of sponsorship. Christmas was approaching and hopefully Santa was bringing a life raft, 80 days' worth of food and a couple of EPIRBs.

12 I'm off to row the Tasman

Well what do I do? I'm 20k short with four days till Christmas and 10 days until Dad arrives in Coffs Harbour to meet me with the boat. I have no plane ticket, no satellite phone and no life raft. TTII is on hold until I can convince someone else I'm a worthy cause. Still I am optimistic and always will be, I believe strongly that something will work and I will find support somewhere, but this does nothing for my stress levels nor does it help with paying the rent. I keep thinking to myself, what is the likelihood of a company looking to purchase advertising on an ocean rowing boat just four days before Christmas? Giving up is not an option so the relentless pursuit continues and today I will find a sponsored lifejacket and also follow up five more organizations who have received my sponsorship proposal.
My diary, 21 December 2009

I had been in this situation so many times over the past two years. Looking back now I'm surprised at how many things just seemed to happen, but only when it came down to the wire. Suddenly, a solution would pop up.

The biggest pressure was Dad arriving in Coffs Harbour. His flights were already booked and I was terrified he'd have to cancel them and lose money because I couldn't get there with the boat in time. I hounded the phones until Christmas Eve, getting the same answers every time. Either the organization had closed for Christmas or they would look at my proposal in their next budget. Accustomed by now to the art of sponsorship refusal, it didn't take much to read between the lines and move on to the next phone call.

The worst aspect was the rise and fall of emotions I experienced as some company or manager would show a glimmer of hope — the possibility of a yes would send me into a tornado of excitement as the door was suddenly swung open only to be slammed shut again. This happened countless times until my proposal reached someone with the scruples to say directly, 'No, we won't be supporting your expedition.'

One particular organization told me they were interested and couldn't see why they wouldn't support me and had the budget for it. I hung out for a response from these guys, eventually tracking them down on Boxing Day to be told they would look into it again in February. I was devastated.

With the commercial world shutting down over the holiday period I thought my next step would be a call to Dad to cancel his flights, then I'd need to find some storage for *TTII* in Sydney while I waited on further sponsorship.

I was down in Taupo, at the bach with Lisa and her family, intermittently taking calls in regards to *TTII* and trying hard to get into the spirit of the season instead of panicking about being away from the Internet and emails. I filled in time taking apart an old watermaker in preparation for what now seemed to be a hopelessly distant Tasman attempt.

Lisa's father, Winton Jones, had always been supportive of my expedition but I was never quite sure what he thought about his daughter being involved with a bloke trying to row the Tasman. If he had any ounce of doubt he did very well in hiding it and always provided insightful comments from his sailing experience. Winton approached me in the bach kitchen, telling me that he and Jill (Lisa's stepmum) would like to help. I responded with an uneasy OK, not really knowing what he meant. They'd already provided so much support that any more was fairly unnecessary. Winton didn't specify what 'help' entailed, so I said thank you and we both moved on.

Somewhat curious, that night I asked Lisa if she had prompted it and what it would entail and she told me Winton and Jill had discussed lending me some money to get to Australia. I was very uneasy with this prospect and felt embarrassed at the idea of borrowing money, especially knowing I had no means of paying it back in the immediate future. The fact that it was a loan from my girlfriend's father added some extra worry to the equation. I thought about this for a few days, racking my brain for other options to get to the start line, until we were all packed up and about to head back to Auckland. Christmas and trout fishing had taken over, and there had been no more talk about the Tasman.

We were about to hop in the car when Winton called me over and wrote me out a cheque — enough to cover my flights and get me to Coffs Harbour. Without a doubt this was a massive turning point; not only was it the financial boost I needed but someone I respected now stood behind me and believed in me.

As I was rowing across the Tasman I would draw on moments such as these as reasons not to give up and to keep persevering; it certainly added to my determination not to let down all the people who had supported me. We left Taupo on Friday afternoon and I would have to wait until Monday to bank my cheque and start looking at flights. With an exciting week-end planned I was able to head out and purchase some new maritime charts and navigation equipment and start studying more ocean navigation. Monday morning I was straight to the bank and then off to book my flight to meet up with Dad in Coffs Harbour. A pretty standard procedure, until the booking agent came to travel insurance and I had to describe what I was up to and what cover I would need. I laughed when I ticked the box on the insurance document indicating cover for water sport injuries and was happy to read that the insurance covered boating activities out to 37 km. Better than nothing I figured, so I signed and walked out with a booking reference to fly to Sydney at 7 a.m. on New Year's Eve.

The next few days flew past and I spent most of them trying to track down a life raft and other equipment. As just about everything was closed this was fruitless and 30 December was upon me before I knew it.

Lisa had loaned me a back pack and had stacked it with around 100 protein bars and energy drink, all of which would eventually be packed into my daily food bags. We also spent some time working out what clothing I was going to take on the expedition and tried to squeeze it in as well.

My flight was at 7.15 a.m. New Zealand time which meant I had to be at the airport by around 5.15 a.m., which is not the best time to say goodbye to the girlfriend. It would have to do as I need as much time as possible in Sydney before the weekend. Before this morning I haven't been upset about what I'm attempting. I've always felt the challenge and tried to step up to it, but leaving Lisa was hard. She'd been there to listen to my troubles and celebrate all the little triumphs, and now she won't be.

My diary, 31 December 2009

I would sometimes wonder if having a girlfriend involved in my preparation had softened me up, but this hadn't been the case. Having a support person is imperative. I hate to sound clichéd, but Lisa was my rock through the last year, the only consistent thing in my life. I will always be grateful for her smile, loud laugh and love.

Arriving in Sydney on New Year's Eve I anticipated the Australian authorities would be preparing to celebrate New Year rather than clear my boat into their country. This was a bit of a worry but I had to be there in person to sort things out. Luckily, it was a normal flight with only a few bumps, which always send my heart rate through the roof. Strangely, I spent most of it trying to convince myself that it's not that far across the Tasman, making whimsical statements about being 30,000 feet up and if I was rowing that high I'd be there much faster. Must have been the nerves.

I landed in Sydney for the first time in my life, grateful to be out of the air and on the ground, beginning my adventure. I hired a car as soon as I arrived and all that I could think of was how I was going to get the boat up to Coffs Harbour, which was a good 690 km away, that same day. The past year had taught me to not expect too much of anything and if something can go wrong 99 times out of 100 it will. Sure enough, Customs hadn't found time to inspect my boat yet and told me because Friday was a public holiday the boat wouldn't be inspected until sometime next week. 'So sorry Shaun, call again the middle of next week.'

It only takes one small thing to derail a project on a tight budget and I would now be in an increasingly expensive limbo until the middle of next week, or whenever Customs made time to inspect my boat. The worst part was the fact that Dad was flying into Coffs Harbour two days from now. I finally had to make the call I'd been dreading, telling him to cancel his flights to Coffs, and that we'd be chilling out in a Sydney hotel for the next five days. Dad had specifically said he didn't like Sydney and wanted to spend as little time there as possible, but this was no longer going to be the case.

By this stage I'd been in Australia for an hour and had set up a mobile phone, hired a car and was driving my way around Sydney, developing a plan about how to use my time effectively. I called Patrick Brothers, from Rush Labs, as he had all my freeze-dried Back Country food, which had been posted to his place. Patrick was the one who had been supporting me since day one, yet I'd never met him. Excited at finally catching up with him, I sent Pat a text and arranged a time to fill my hire car with food and, more importantly, meet him face to face and thank him for his support.

Pat lived close to Darling Harbour and I eventually navigated my way to his apartment, where he greeted me at the gate. It was wonderful to finally meet him and also vent some of my frustration about Customs keeping my boat until next week, and brainstorming a few ideas around how to get to Coffs. After about an hour or so of chatting the car was loaded and Pat had decided a media release would be a good idea. Perhaps Dad and I could fill some time in Sydney doing a few media interviews to hopefully get some help to sort out the last few missing pieces.

I left Pat's not really having anywhere to go. I'd always wanted to visit the northern beaches and drive over the Sydney Harbour Bridge, so set out on a small Sydney adventure. That afternoon I had set some time aside to call Dad and tell him I couldn't get the boat, and the worst part was that he probably wouldn't get to see it if Customs didn't release it before Wednesday, when he had to head back to work. Not an easy call to make. Not because I was worried about Dad's reaction, but more because I was feeling as though I had failed him in some way. Of course Dad reacted fine and cancelled his connecting flight from Sydney to Coffs Harbour without any trouble. He'd be arriving in two days.

After my reconnaissance of Sydney it was nearly 4 p.m. and I needed to arrange some accommodation for the night. A few weeks earlier I was emailed by an old friend, Dean Story, who worked in Sydney and had offered to help out. I got hold of Dean on the phone and he kindly offered me his couch for as long as I wanted. Dean had no big night planned so we happily shared a few beers at his place before having a relatively early night.

I was woken up early by a phone call from ABC Television wanting to arrange an interview with me and Dad over the next few days. A little jaded from the beers the night before I managed to lock in a time, and this was quickly followed by another call from Channel 7 News, wanting to know if Dad and I would go on the breakfast programme and when we would be available.

As the day went on I ended up fielding around 20 radio interviews and requests for either magazine articles or television interviews; most people also wanted to see the boat, which increased my frustration with not being able to gain access for another few days.

The media attention reinforced that what I was doing was interesting — for so long I battled to get coverage in New Zealand and now I was struggling to keep up with the media's expectations. Dad would have even more trouble remaining enthusiastic, with his general reluctance to appear on camera or take part in any interviews. He flew in to Sydney airport at about 2 p.m. and I had booked us in to meet with Patrick and record a few interviews before I left that could be used while I was out at sea.

The trip from the airport to Pat's place gave me a good hour in the car with Dad to catch up on a few things and let him know about the hold-up with Customs. The interviews with Patrick were quite insightful as he questioned Dad about his experiences on the Tasman and what Dad thought I was in for. I listened very carefully when he talked about the frightening things that could happen.

I had booked us into a hotel in the middle of Darling Harbour, as we needed to be in the city for interviews and Dad and I couldn't couch surf the entire time. I also needed the hotel to establish a base to operate from, with Internet and phone facilities, to give myself the best chance of getting *TTII* released from Customs and somehow rounding up a free life raft.

We completed an interview on Sunrise this morning, quite funny watching Dad get some make-up put on — we shared the make-up room with some woman who was loudly swearing down her phone in the 2-metre by 3-metre room we were sharing. She looked like a witch and sounded like one. Channel 7 interview went well, had a good chat to Mark and Mel, the hosts, but forgot to mention that I needed a few things like 20k — I must remember to mention sponsorship on every occasion.

My diary, 4 January 2010

Dad came across really well in interviews and it was great to be able to rely on him to be able to do this so well. I wasn't that honest with him sometimes — when he would ask how many people were watching the show, instead of letting him know there were about two million, to ease his nerves I'd tell him it was more like a few thousand. For a few days our routine would be based around fitting in as many media opportunities as possible, followed by staying in the hotel room hunting sponsorship and putting pressure on Customs to clear my boat.

After the major media interviews I was emailed with offers of support, the strangest being an Australian bloke who told me I could have a free clothesline from his shop, which was about all he could offer, but he wanted to wish me good luck!

Along with other offers of support came one from a man called Steven Gates, who had previously rowed the Tasman in a crew of four, from Hokianga Harbour to Sydney. Steve had contacted me seven months earlier, offering to help me out if I needed it. I'd replied to him at the time but had completely forgotten his offer. Steve got in touch and invited Dad and me round to his place for dinner with his family. We eventually tracked down Steve's house, where we were treated to some fantastic Aussie hospitality. I was well and truly welcomed to Sydney, with a few bottles of champagne being consumed and Tasman Sea rowing banter being thrown around as Dad and Steve compared notes and tall tales.

Steve put plenty of concerns to rest for me when he let me in on his philosophy for expedition preparation, this being 'coffee, cigarettes and visualization'. It was quite refreshing hearing his relaxed, laid-back perspective on crossing the Tasman, instilling in me a small but growing sense of confidence that it was going to be OK. We discussed general concerns about what

I needed and without hesitation Steve not only offered to lend me his satellite phone but said he'd also drive me and the boat to Coffs Harbour *and* let me have the use of his warehouse in Sydney to complete the final adjustments to *TTII*.

I drove away from his place feeling as though I had absolutely hit the jackpot. Not once in my entire planning did I think that so many important aspects would fall into place just like that; his generosity ticked off a number of the major challenges that still needed sorting.

Back in the hotel I had my first good night's sleep in Aussie, only to be woken at around 4.45 a.m. by a New Zealand breakfast radio station wanting an interview, which I didn't actually mind. With all the good news that had developed the night before I bragged about my progress accordingly.

Steve offered to take me to Coffs Harbour on the Sunday. Dad was booked to fly back to Darwin on the Wednesday before, so it was now clear he wouldn't get to see me off, and the way things were going he probably wouldn't even get to see the boat.

With only a couple of days to go before Dad was booked to leave, the mornings were full of phone calls to Customs, but it was the same response each time. They had booked in to clear the boat on Wednesday afternoon and there was no reason for them to clear it any earlier. Frustrated as hell, I decided that if Dad wasn't going to be there when I left Australia then it would be good to spend a bit of relaxed time together among the chaos. This was the most amount of time I had spent with Dad for a long time, so we did some sightseeing around Sydney which helped fill in the gaps.

Wednesday arrived and I called to receive the news that Customs had released my boat and it would be available at 2 p.m. — the only problem with this was that 2 p.m. was exactly when Dad needed to check in for his flight back to Darwin. This made the logistics tight, but I was determined he was going to see *TTII* before he went back up north, to make his trip to Sydney worthwhile.

I called Steve who was on standby with his Land Cruiser and told him to meet us at the Customs clearance point just before the 2 p.m. deadline. Dad had packed up his gear and in a nice surprise for me had paid the hotel bill for both of us. Feeling excited but a little stressed due to the time pressure, we made our way over to the Customs pick-up yard only to find a queue of about 45 trucks in front of us. Immediately thinking the worst, I was filled with disappointment and pulled into the car park of the building next door to wait for Steve. As the clock ticked away there were only a few minutes before we needed to drop Dad at the airport.

I thought that maybe we could get in around the back of the building we were parked in front of, so in a final touch of excitement to brighten Dad's otherwise lacklustre Sydney experience, we went round the back and found a beautiful hole in the fence. In a fantastic moment of triumph I saw *TTII* parked only a few metres away and Dad had a good five-minute inspection before Steve arrived, ready to take him to the airport.

It was a fairly rushed and unemotional goodbye and good luck from Dad. I felt a bit disappointed about coming so frustratingly close to being able to go for a row with Dad in Sydney Harbour, but I had to be happy that he got to see the boat at all.

I headed back to Customs with Steve to fetch *TTII*, very excited to finally get my hands on her again. While Steve started to remove the space-saver tyre I went to deal with the paperwork. I ended up taking 45 minutes to work through all the forms and sign all the necessary documents before heading back out to where Steve had the wheel on and was starting to pack everything up for the trip to his warehouse.

It was 4 p.m. when Steve reversed up to *TTII* and I lifted the trailer up only to find that the tow ball was too big. Once again I was so close and yet so far, and dealing with this one was going to be no small mission. With Customs closing soon the heat was on to get to the local Repco auto parts centre to find a new tow ball. Repco was out of stock and our only option was to remove the coupling from Steve's work trailer and attach it to my trailer. This was all done over a couple of hours and we ended up having to drill a few new holes in my trailer and clip it onto the Land Cruiser to finally get *TTII* out of Customs and into Steve's warehouse.

It was nearly 8 p.m. by the time she was inside; Steve and I were exhausted and ready for a few beers. By this stage Tim, Steve's best mate, had arrived from Tasmania and we settled in for an evening of tall stories and plenty of beers, eventually getting the slug gun from downstairs and having target practice in the backyard at around midnight.

Residing on the couch for the night, I took time to flick through some of Steve's formidable collection of ocean rowing books, even though we had a big drive the next day up to Coffs, and a solid amount of work to be done on the boat before we left.

Everyone was up early. I needed to catch up with Patrick and collect a few more pieces of equipment from the middle of Sydney before I headed up north, so Steve and Tim left to make a head start on getting the boat ready. I took about two hours to get sorted and slowly navigate my way around Sydney, arriving back at Steve's warehouse to find the guys had almost finished. They'd built me a safety line, reattached the wheel arches and connected the watermaker. *TTII* was almost ready to roll! Tim had also made me a couple of safety harnesses to use while rowing and Steve donated a lifejacket/safety harness to use on the expedition. One o'clock ticked around and it was time to head up to Coffs.

I just needed to drop off my rental car at Kings Cross and we would be on our way. I nervously followed Steve as he drove my pride and joy out of the car park. My next stop was to deliver the rental car without any scratches, which thankfully I managed to do, only a little bitter at the $500 immediately sucked out of my bank account — it was a necessary but painful cost.

Rental car delivered, I jumped into the back of the Land Cruiser to begin the adventure north, stopping first at a boat shop to collect a few bits and pieces, such as spare shackles and stainless bolts and then slogging it out a solid four or so hours until we reached the first McDonald's and treated ourselves. With a few more hours to go it was verging on dusk, around 7.30 p.m., and I saw a few wild kangaroos bouncing around the place, reminding me that I wasn't at home and wouldn't be for some time. I started to miss home a bit as I realized that Steve and Tim would head off soon and I would be back to operating on my own again.

13 Coffs Harbour

It was 11 p.m. before we pulled up outside a restaurant on the main strip in Coffs Harbour. The first thing I noticed when I stepped out was the heat and humidity, thinking straight away about how this was going to affect my rowing. All the restaurant patrons stared over at the strange-looking red boat on the back as I frantically rummaged through my gear looking for directions to the motel.

I couldn't find the information or the handwritten notes on where I was staying — all I could remember was that the road it was on started with Beach so we drove around for about half an hour hunting for this 'Beach Road'. Luckily, Coffs is a small place and it didn't take us too long to eventually track down the motel. With a huge lack of car parking space the next big challenge was where on earth we were going to put the boat for the night.

Steve reversed the Land Cruiser as far as he could and we unclipped *TTII* and manoeuvred her nicely in between a wall and another car, taking out a few small palm trees in the process. It would certainly do for the next few nights. We all paused for a moment once the boat was in the car park.

By now it was about midnight and the guys had been working on the boat all morning, driven us up to Coffs and now were about to drive back home. There was no way I could thank them enough for what they had done and without them I doubt I'd have made it to the start line.

With time against them I managed to get one quick photo of the guys before they disappeared back to Sydney. It was 1 a.m. and after a bit of sleep I would be spending my first day in Coffs Harbour — my boat and I were finally here. With no one around to celebrate with, I phoned Lisa to let her know I'd arrived and shared a celebratory moment with her before going to sleep.

The sun was up and so was I, heading off for my first reconnaissance mission to Coffs Harbour. I headed straight down to the beach and along to the yacht club, to check out the scene and hopefully recruit some helpers.

My first port of call was the boat-building yard, as when I was still in Sydney I'd spoken to a guy up here called Ray, asking if I could work on my boat in his yard while I was in Coffs, hoping he'd let me keep her there for free. Strolling around the boat yard, Ray was nowhere to be seen, so I ended up chatting to a guy in the yacht club next door, who told me Ray had gone away for a week. Yet another minor setback, but as there were plenty of other jobs to be done this wasn't a problem. I was more concerned about what the motel would say about having the boat in their car park for a week.

My next task was to look at where exactly I would be rowing. Dad had always told me the most dangerous parts of the expedition would be the departure and the landing, so I was curious to get a good look at what was ahead of me, for the first few days of rowing at least.

At the entrance to Coffs there's a decent-sized hill called Muttonbird Island, with a fantastic view of the entire harbour, where I'd be able to suss out any potential risks. From the peak I immediately noticed a collection of small islands, both north and south of the harbour entrance, and about 2 km offshore. They weren't posing any sort of threat, but I knew it would be important to avoid being blown onto them when I left.

Apart from avoiding the islands off the coast, departure seemed relatively simple; the only other threats I could think of were the shipping lanes, which were around 28 km offshore, and the fact that there were a lot of whales and marine life around the harbour entrance.

Plaguing my mind the entire time was money. I only had enough for a few more days in the motel and I still needed a life raft and some other fairly highly priced items, so I headed home to start emailing and phoning potential last-minute sponsors.

I was also exhausted after spending most of the day wandering around in the heat; this was slightly worrying because of what I was going to be doing in the next few months, but I was sure I would acclimatize. The next day I needed to track down some decent hardware stores for equipment on the boat, including various types of rope, flares, stainless-steel nuts and bolts, most of my food and a portable GPS unit as a back-up navigation system.

With the shopping list in front of me I grabbed a map from reception and started walking towards the main centre. After a few hours wandering around I tracked down the main industrial supply centre, which looked as if it had enough shops to supply me with most of what I needed. It was always quite funny purchasing items as the usual question most salespeople ask is, 'What are you using it for?' The response on a good day would usually end up with some sort of discount, but if I wasn't in the mood I would make up a more boring purpose and just move on.

It was the same routine for the next three or four days, sourcing all the different things I needed to finish off the boat and waiting for Ray the boat builder to get back so I could move the boat. Each evening I'd be on the phone to media or life-raft suppliers trying to convince them to either lend or give me a life raft.

I'd been in Coffs Harbour for five days and the excitement of being there had worn off. I'd made some progress and had some more equipment, but without the life raft I didn't have an expedition and I was starting to feel a bit down.

I woke up the next day to check my emails, and found a forwarded message from one of Lisa's friends, who just happened to be living in Coffs Harbour. Anna had emailed Lisa letting her know that she and her husband Mark were going away for a couple of weeks. Their apartment would be empty, so we were welcome to use it! Another absolute godsend had just fallen into my lap. I called Anna and Mark to take them up on their generous offer, and arrange a time for a coffee and to thank them in person. Lisa was landing the next day and we would only need to spend one day in the motel before moving into the apartment, which would provide all we needed to sort out gear and host the support team, which was also about to arrive.

Before we moved into Anna and Mark's apartment I was able to borrow a truck to get the boat down to the yard, as Ray had returned and I could finally get stuck into the last important jobs before launching *TTII*.

Lisa arrived, which was awesome, and great for her to be able to arrive in an environment where for once I had a couple of things sorted out. Not that this would last long, but hopefully she had a nice first day in Coffs Harbour. At this early stage I was eyeing up Monday, 18 January as my departure day and the long-term weather was looking OK, but I still had to check with my weather man.

Weather was going to be a massive component of my Tasman crossing and if it didn't go my way it could certainly mean the end of my expedition. I was incredibly ignorant when it came to weather and really knew very little about the different systems I could be facing. For a while I thought that even if I did know what was happening with the weather, with my lack of ability to do anything about it maybe ignorance would be more relaxing than knowing a storm was coming.

In 2008 I watched James Castrission and Justin Jones kayak the Tasman together and I was curious as to how they had approached weather information and who had helped them. I made a few phone calls and read about their expedition and I was introduced to the name Rodger Badham, aka Clouds. It didn't take long after typing his name into Google to figure out that Clouds was clearly one of the best people I could hope to have on my team for help with the weather.

Clouds' CV included a number of round-the-world yacht races and he was currently working with the Team New Zealand America's Cup syndicate and also helping the Ferrari Formula One race team. After reading through this I thought I'd have no hope of getting his help, but nonetheless I gave him a phone call to see how he reacted if I tried my luck.

My introduction on the phone started awkwardly.

'My name is Shaun Quincey and I'm rowing the Tasman this year.'

Clouds let out a little chuckle.

My next question was, 'So when do you think a good time to go would be?'

Clouds reply? 'Never!'

We shared a few emails and phone calls as the year went on and I got closer and closer to leaving for Australia. I would discuss the Tasman with him but was never really sure if he was willing to come on board as 'Weather Man' for the expedition.

With about a week to go Clouds happened to be on a family holiday about 60 km south of where I was staying at Coffs Harbour and I called him to let him know I was thinking of leaving on Monday afternoon. He told me he would be travelling up the coast in the next few days and we could discuss the weather reporting then.

I would finally get to meet my weather man a few days before I left to cross the Tasman. Clouds arrived in Coffs and not only provided an incredible insight into the Tasman's currents and weather patterns, but also agreed to text-message me the weather twice a day to inform me of oncoming weather. Clouds became an absolutely integral member of Team Tasman and I would rely heavily on the weather information he would text to me each day.

With a departure date in mind the countdown had officially begun and the job list started to grow exponentially as Lisa and I looked at everything that still needed to be done. Without launching into a panic, the next week was all about making haste and trying to enjoy our last time together for a while, as well as track down the final pieces of essential equipment.

Each day started with a visit down to the boat to check that whatever painting or resin work I'd done the day before had dried. This would move on to the next job as Lisa passed me tools or took the piss about how sweaty I was getting when I wasn't even rowing. We'd then head out to the shops and round up what we could.

By about Wednesday it was clear that without something dramatic changing there was no way I was going to be leaving on Monday. We didn't have all the food I needed, no life raft or sea anchors — all of which were vital — and there was still a few days' work needed to complete the boat.

We got home around 7 p.m., utterly exhausted and with our relationship fully tested, to find a collection of messages. The first was to tell us that Winton and Jill had decided to come over and help out and would be arriving tomorrow. The second was from Michael and Olly, who were looking at flights at the weekend, and the last one from my cousin Paul and his son Ethan, who were arriving tomorrow from Brisbane.

When it rains it certainly pours and I couldn't believe how things had swung around with a few phone calls. More than a little emotional and a bit teary eyed, Lisa and I took a few beers down to the pool to celebrate. With the Kiwi contingent slowly making their way over, there was an opportunity to approach sponsors to get some more gear sent over packed into their bags — in particular the Coppins sea anchors, probably one of the most essential pieces of equipment for the crossing.

I'd arranged for the anchors (a larger anchor and a smaller drogue) to be made in New Zealand and Coppins were still in the process of figuring out how to get them to me before

Monday. I called Coppins Sea Anchors, letting them know Winton and Jill's flight details. They managed to throw the anchors into an overnight courier, which reached Winton and Jill just in time to pack for their flight.

The next day Paul and his son Ethan showed up. I hadn't seen Paul since his son Joshua's funeral a year or so earlier, so it was good to catch up with him and I was stoked he'd made the effort. Along with Ethan, Paul had also brought his truck, which was essential for launching the boat. I'd arranged some media to follow us down to the boat ramp and Ethan made his TV debut going for a ride across the harbour into the Coffs marina as I rowed *TTII* for the first time in two weeks. Paul and Ethan could only stay for a brief visit and left early the next day, this being the day Winton and Jill arrived with my sea anchors.

I couldn't wait for the anchors so I could get out into the harbour and begin some much needed testing. Lisa went to pick up Winton and Jill from the airport while I stayed put, firing off a few more emails in a last desperate attempt to track down a life raft.

Scrolling through the local directory I found Great Circle Life Rafts, who were based in Brisbane, only a few hundred kilometres north, and decided to call them. Paul Montgomery, the owner, answered the phone. I told him my story and that I only had a few days left. Paul told me to call him back in a day as he wanted time to think about how exactly he was going to get a 30 kg life raft to me.

Paul called me early the next morning to tell me a yacht was sailing back after completing the Sydney to Hobart race. They'd borrowed a life raft and would be calling into Coffs Harbour to refuel. All I had to do was promise to wait until the courier had delivered some stickers to put on the boat, sign a few bits of paper and the life raft was mine for the journey. Once again luck had fallen on my side and one more essential box was ticked — all I had to do was rendezvous with the yacht and the huge life-raft burden would be gone.

That night I had a phone call from Dad asking me where I was staying. I told him about the apartment and he said that was a bloody shame because he was having a few beers in the motel I had just moved from!

Another great surprise. Dad had thrown in work for a few days to fly down from Darwin with his wife, Nitaya. Lisa and I shot down to the motel and we had a couple of beers and planned the next few days. I was starting to feel as if I had a team behind me, especially when Michael and Olly arrived at 2 a.m. after driving down from Brisbane Airport.

The last few major jobs were packing the food, reinstalling the watermaker and sorting out what the weather was doing, which would involve a meeting with Clouds, all of which would have to happen over the next two days. My job now was to coordinate Team Tasman, which had just grown from Lisa and me to a crew of eight.

With room for only two people on the boat at a time, Michael and Olly were reinstalling the watermaker, Lisa and Jill were off to the supermarket to buy food and first-aid supplies, while Dad and Nitaya went to the hardware store to find some type of sunshade. If we were all at home these jobs would take no time at all, but because none of us had ever been to Coffs before, every little job would take hours as you slowly found the right people to help with each job.

During this process Winton and I collected ropes and parachute flares. The first day with Team Tasman went well and we achieved what would have been impossible with just the two of us. Lisa and Jill had managed to pick up 80 days' worth of supplies for me, taking them in and out of supermarkets for most of the day as they bargained for the best discounts and deals, and they were exhausted.

We'd decided earlier on that day to have a barbecue, and it turned into a slightly premature departure party. I guess I would describe the evening as a collection of personalities that in any other environment would probably never get the opportunity to sit down and have a meal together. Both the absolute uniqueness of the situation and the fact I was about to row the bloody Tasman struck me as I sat at one end of the table sharing beers with Michael, happily listening to voices I wouldn't hear for some time.

It was Sunday morning and I wanted to leave the next day. Lisa and Jill were packing food into individual bags, creating daily food packs and I was waiting for Clouds to arrive. We were all keen to hear what he'd have to say about my timing and the all-important weather forecast.

When he arrived around 10 a.m. the apartment was looking like a sweatshop, with the girls rushing around in a food-packing production line and all sorts of equipment covering the floor.

We made some space and Clouds set up his collection of computers. Straight to the point, he told me the weather was not at all good for a Monday departure, and I should wait till at least Wednesday. This would be my first practical introduction to the changing nature of the Tasman and dealing with its uncontrollable temper.

I was disappointed, as were the rest of the team, because, as there was no chance any of them would be able to stay that long, this meant it would be only me and Lisa on departure day. Everyone gathered around as Clouds discussed the crossing and the various routes I could find myself on and also the adversity I could face.

Up until this point I'd avoided talking about how long I thought it was going to take, not wanting to tempt fate by suggesting I would arrive after a certain number of days, but meeting Clouds was too tempting and I asked the inevitable question.

'How long do you think it will take?'

'Well … the machine predicts it will take you twenty-one days, averaging one knot every twenty-four hours.'

Surprised at this, I waited for the next instalment.

'But Shaun, that doesn't include the possibilities of strong easterly winds and adverse wave direction. That could add another fifty days.'

The reason I had always steered clear of talking about predicted crossing time was out in the open. The Tasman was unpredictable.

At least Cloud's 21-day projection with the possibility of another 50 days on top of that made sure I avoided any guessing game and just got on with the rowing.

The meeting with Clouds was essential and meant that everyone would be kept in the loop with the all-important weather while I was at sea. Clouds and I also established a daily communication routine, which would involve a text message on my satellite phone at both 8 a.m. and 8 p.m., outlining what weather I should expect, which he would then email to all of the land crew. After I'd read this message I would call Michael to provide my coordinates and give him a rating out of 10 for how I was feeling mentally and physically, closely followed by a bit of friendly banter to keep me feeling normal. Clouds' visit lasted only a few hours but it was worth its weight in gold and over the course of the expedition he played one of the most important roles in getting me across.

Dad had to leave shortly and fly back home with Nitaya. I'd really appreciated their visit and the effort he'd gone to in building a sunshade for the boat and generally just being there. He still hadn't taken the boat for a row and I told him he'd just have to wait until I got back home.

The girls had finished packing the food into the bags so Lisa, Winton and Jill decided to go on a tour of Coffs Harbour for the afternoon while Michael, Olly and I headed down to the boat to make sure the watermaker was running smoothly and a few other systems were functioning OK.

Another day down and Team Tasman was slowly shrinking, as Dad and Nitaya had left and Olly and Michael were about to head off early the next morning. I desperately wanted them to stay around for my departure, very conscious of the fact that there would be no one there for Lisa once I rowed off, but nothing could be done about this — it was just the reality of the situation.

Very early on Monday morning Olly and Michael shot up north and it was now just the four of us in the apartment, everyone aware there were only two days until I left. The life raft had arrived the previous day and fitted perfectly into its allocated slot and there was only a handful of minor jobs left.

Winton and Jill were flying out that afternoon and we managed to pack the car up to the top of the windows with supplies to take down to *TTII* for the voyage. Food for 80 days, first-aid equipment, clothing, electronics, spare water — there was enough to fill three supermarket trolleys.

It was a bit awkward trying to find places for it all in the limited storage compartments, which weren't huge, and we also had to make sure that when we finished, the boat would still be balanced for rowing. Once the boat was all packed up I had a few hours to take her out with Winton and play around with the sea anchors and test her balance. I ran through a few routines and I could feel how the handling had changed with the increased weight.

Later, it was time to take Winton and Jill to the airport. I was so glad they'd come over, I'm not sure what I would have done without their support — and it was a very stressful time for Lisa, so I was glad she had someone to talk to about it all.

A completely hectic and full-on few days had resulted in most of the jobs being completed in time and I was ready to row the Tasman. I decided not to spend much time with *TTII* on my last day, as I had no idea how long I was going to be living on her, so we only made one quick visit. We had some New Zealand media show up for an interview at the apartment and I made sure the various media outlets knew I was leaving the next day. I also sent a few emails acknowledging the support I'd received from sponsors and thanked them before turning the phone off and reflecting on the past two years.

Lisa prepared a wonderful meal — steak and potatoes with a stack of fresh vegetables — my last home-cooked meal for the foreseeable future. It was hard to believe my battle to make it to the start line was just about over and the huge adventure, which had dominated my life for the past two years, was finally about to start. I was exactly where I'd dreamed of being, yet, surprisingly, I felt almost flat, and I was amazed at my lack of joy and enthusiasm. What was wrong with me?

Looking back now, I can see that I was shit scared of letting everyone down, and a bit awed thinking about all the help I'd had in making it this far. I desperately didn't want to disappoint any of those amazing people. The last thing I wanted to do was let my team down and while I knew I'd slogged my guts out getting here in a figurative sense, the next few months would be the real thing. I was now going to have to put in some serious physical effort and there would be no one else out there to help me pull on those oars, that's for sure.

But this wasn't the night for uncertainty and nerves — I wanted to make sure Lisa was at ease with what was about to happen and the pressure she would be under as well. We'd planned and talked about worst-case scenarios and the role she would have to play in dealing with the media if I went missing.

Death was never discussed, as we both never saw it as a possibility. I never really allowed the prospect of death to enter my thoughts. I left Coffs Harbour without having made a will, as in my mind there was no need for one. Everything I owned was in my boat and I decided against leaving Lisa with a letter to read if I died. Slightly selfish in hindsight, as if I had died I would have left quite a mess for others to try to tidy up, but I didn't want to even entertain the idea and leave myself open to the possibility of death entering the picture. In a strange way I would tell myself that I couldn't die because there was nothing in place to deal with this possibility and I absolutely needed to get home to ensure I could be responsible for the various obligations I had waiting there. I did, however, fear death and this certainly drove a significant amount of my extra planning and precautionary measures. It also meant I was incredibly stringent about having the appropriate safety equipment and that people knew exactly where I was 24 hours a day in case things ever got really serious.

In my final email I made the following note to all rescue authorities and support crew:

If communication stops <u>this is not</u> an indication of trouble or assistance required. The two EPIRBs are the only indication of assistance required and I would be grateful if this was adhered to for a minimum of 50 days after the last communication is received. There is an EPIRB attached to me at all times.

I was ready for my adventure to begin. The alarm was set for 7 a.m. and tomorrow I would start to row the Tasman.

14 The first stroke

I woke up around 5 a.m. with my number-one supporter lying next to me, happily asleep. I'd kept the phone turned off overnight, as the media didn't seem to care much for sleep patterns. Lying in bed staring at the ceiling, I reflected whether this was the right path for me. Should I really step into that boat today, I wondered, coming up with a hundred reasons why I shouldn't.

I had never really considered not doing it before, but right now it was hard to silence the small voices of apprehension eating away at my confidence. I found myself outside checking the wind, standing on the front lawn of the apartment. I could see my Tasman. Today she was smooth and, just as Clouds had predicted, we had a smooth southwesterly of about 10 knots, Hopefully, this would blow me exactly where I wanted to go once I left the mouth of the harbour. I took out my compass and rechecked the direction. Sure enough, it was a southwesterly breeze. I took a few moments alone on the lawn, thinking that at this time tomorrow I would have spent my first night on the Tasman Sea. I quietly reassured myself that I was ready to say goodbye to what was normal and attack what a lot of people said would be impossible.

I walked inside to wake Lisa and enjoy our last few moments of normality by sharing a nice cup of filter coffee on the porch, something I'd definitely miss while out at sea. As we sipped our coffee and silently stared out at the Tasman, we both knew there was a lot still to do, but neither of us wanted to end these last few moments together.

The best-case scenario for me would have been to be rowing out of Coffs Harbour as the sun was rising, to get as much daytime rowing as possible. The reason for this was simple — all the container ships and fishing boats could see me, and I could get substantially clear of land and avoid the risk of being swept back onto the coast or rocks before I stopped rowing for the night.

Unfortunately, the morning was full of jobs and Team Tasman was down to just me and Lisa. The morning started off with a bit of cleaning — after all, we'd had six people staying at the apartment and we needed to tidy the place. This was important as I wasn't happy about the idea of me rowing off into the blue and Lisa coming back to clean by herself. As soon as we'd finished, we loaded up the car with all of the last-minute stuff I hadn't wanted to leave out and left for the boat, after a final meal of scrambled eggs on toast.

During the clean-up I fielded around 20 phone calls from New Zealand and Australian media, all wanting to know departure times and asking a whole lot of what felt to me like very intrusive questions, none of which I wanted to hear and all along the lines of death and did I think I was going to make it. The *New Zealand Herald* asked me whether I felt motivated and if so what was motivating me.

I said that it didn't really matter whether I was motivated or not, I still had to row the bloody thing and my philosophy was as simple as that. It hadn't been done before in this direction;

140

my dad was the first to do it from New Zealand and I sure as hell wasn't going to let anyone else be the first the other way.

Soon, the car was packed, we'd locked up the apartment, I'd stopped answering the phone and we were on our way to the marina. As we were driving a strange sensation of being extra aware of the things I took for granted came over me, and I found myself taking in my surroundings with a little more gratitude, probably in anticipation of not having any of them around for a while. As we drove through the town centre past the camping shop where Olly had bought my cooking gas, then past the rubber store where I'd found the bungee cords to hold down the life raft, everything seemed a bit surreal. The marina was only a 10-minute drive from the apartment, so within no time we were there. Lisa dropped me and a few bags of kit just next door to Customs, so I could sign out of Australia. The blokes there had been great and very supportive of the expedition, and we quickly went through the standard departure process, with them checking my passport and making sure I wasn't exporting anything illegal.

Passport stamped, I walked down the stairs and saw *TTII* floating where I'd left her the day before, a New Zealand flag flying high on top of the main VHF aerial. It was a seriously cool moment, and I was incredibly proud to call her my home for the next few months. Even if I only rowed a few kilometres offshore I felt in some small way that just getting to the start line was an achievement to celebrate.

For a few moments it was just me and *TTII* on the wharf together, a small taste of what was to come. It didn't take long for TVNZ and TV3 from New Zealand to arrive, as well as ABC and Channel 7 Australia. I thought for a few moments there would be some squabbling, but they all managed to squeeze

141

onto the wharf together, where they ended up having to wait for some time. Being optimistic, I'd told the media to be there at 8.30 a.m. on the dot in order to catch my departure, but after we arrived I realized it was going to take us some time to pack the main cabin, fill the tanks with water and generally just sort stuff out on board, so I ended up making the poor buggers wait for nearly two hours.

It was 10 a.m. on 20 January 2010, the wind started to shift a little to the left and I had my departing westerly. With the boat still tied to the wharf, I stepped off *TTII* onto the concrete floating platform, where I changed into my rowing clothing, watched by about 100 locals and a collection of TV crews. I was wondering how Lisa was going to cope with them all by herself after I rowed off, but there was no time for any more stalling. My boat was ready and my adventure was now just one step away.

'Well, time to get on with it.' As I hugged Lisa goodbye the last 18 months of struggle flashed past and I broke down in tears, and I still don't know if they were tears of joy that I'd made it to the start line, or tears of sadness because I was leaving. I have never felt more aware of my place in the world, or what was important than at that exact moment. Gathering a bit of composure after my sobbing uselessness, I was extremely grateful for my treasured sponsored sunglasses, which were currently hiding the volumes of tears. The media swooped in for my final thoughts, and I sensed they were still hunting for any sign of last-minute reservations. I happily gave them nothing but calm confidence, saying there was a job to do, and I had all the tools I needed to do it.

With Lisa's help I untied *TTII* from the wharf, stepped in

and sat in my rowing seat. Lisa pushed the boat away from the wharf. With the subtle westerly pushing me back into the wharf I needed to start rowing. My first stroke was followed by a small round of applause from the onlookers, the first time I'd really noticed the crowd. I gave a small wave and saw the Customs officer taking a photo of me rowing out — I suppose as proof of departure.

TTII felt like a ton of bricks exiting the harbour, and I counted through the first 100 strokes the way we did when we were racing surfboats. I realized very quickly that it would be hard to count my strokes all the way across and promptly stopped. A sea kayaker was following me out and we chatted as we exited the harbour together. I relished the company, as I knew it was going to be the last for some time. He was soon replaced by a boat the TV crews had chartered to follow me out. I was quickly reminded of the effect of the wind on *TTII* as I kept being blown into the path of the three-storey, 60-foot launch and was quite relieved when they said their goodbyes as the skipper slowly turned around and headed back. I could see a small figure standing on the rocks forming the break wall to the harbour entrance, and recognized the T-shirt. It was Lisa, and I shed a few more tears, feeling guilty I had left her to deal with this on her own.

Tasman Trespasser II was on her way to New Zealand, and the Tasman was about to begin its assault on my crossing. The most dangerous part of ocean rowing is always departure and landing, due to the sheer number of unmanageable risks — all the things you can't control. Increased shipping activity around coastlines, recreational and commercial fishing boats, container ships, steeper waves due to the shallower bottom and, of course, rocks all pose a significant threat.

Stroke after stroke I looked at Coffs Harbour on the horizon. The 36-degree heat there was horrific and I'd already downed three litres of water. I'd just finished my first couple of hours of rowing and Coffs Harbour still seemed to be in the same bloody place, not disappearing nearly as fast as it had seemed to do in the first 30 minutes! At this early stage I was using my manual compass to navigate and had set my bearings the night before to preserve time. I wanted to clear 56 km on the first day to get past the shipping lanes in daylight.

I continued to row, with old blisters from training cracking open on my hands and weeping onto the oar handles. When I glanced up at the New Zealand flag on the aerial I noticed it was flying in a slightly different direction than when I had departed.

Surely not, I thought to myself. The weather had been pretty much guaranteed to hold some element of westerly wind for the first couple of days, and I'd delayed my departure because I needed a westerly to get off the coast. Sliding the oars inboard I got out my hand compass and immediately felt restricted by my tether lines. I tasted the first temptation to quickly unclip so I could move more freely around the boat, but a quick reflection on the consequences pulled me back in line. So to speak.

Looking down at the compass there had been a definite change in wind direction, right around the clock. I was now going to be rowing straight into a 5- to 10-knot northeasterly. It dawned on me that this was the first of many tests and there was no one to complain to, no buck to pass, just the beginning of a fight between me and the Tasman, with a failed expedition being the result if I lost. With no concept of fairness, the

Tasman was blowing NE, which would push me straight back towards Australia if I didn't row my guts out.

I thought about heading back to shore and waiting for better wind, but decided to take it on the chin as the first test of character. It was as if the Tasman was sounding me out, in the way that boxers exchange insults before a boxing match. My speed had been knocked back by two-thirds and my goal of 56 km and clearing the shipping lanes was going to be well out of reach. Hour after hour I rowed, thinking about what to do that night — including the thought of a potential collision smashing my boat.

On to my fifth litre of water and into my fifth hour of rowing I thought I'd have a look at my distance rowed, even though I knew that every moment I stopped I'd be heading back towards Australia. Oars pulled in I leaned forward to turn on the chart plotter, the device I would use to navigate across, only to see that the small dot used to show my position on the digital screen hadn't moved a millimetre. When I zoomed fully into the image I saw that over five hours of rowing I had moved just over 7 km, putting my speed at an average of 0.8 knots for the day. This would also be the beginning of the dreaded guesstimated countdown of how many days it would take to cross the ditch. The first calculation I made, based on an average of what I'd achieved in the first five hours, would give me about 15 km per day, which equalled 207 days to cross the Tasman. Not the most pleasant thought, considering I had only 80 days' worth of food. I kept rowing.

I was now officially the furthest out to sea I had ever been on my own. The east coast of Australia looked slightly distorted, due to the heat rising from the land, and I could see the odd fishing boat shooting across the water. I had also officially never been so scared or unsure of anything in my entire life. Why had I decided to row the Tasman and why exactly was it so important to achieve when life at home was so good? I loved New Zealand and the way things had been going at home were great. Is it really worth risking my life and missing out on a lifetime?

The sun was setting and I was joined by a pod of curious dolphins, which circled around me, the first of the beautifully unique moments I would experience throughout the crossing. The sky was on fire and I had some guests for the evening. Although I was still dealing with the answer-less question of what the next two months would have in store for me, I embraced the freedom and excitement of my dream beginning.

When the sun disappeared along with the dolphins, I had just completed my seventh hour of rowing, ticking up almost 19 km. Dew had already started to form all over the boat and I was surprised how quickly the sun's heat disappeared. Excited at the prospect of rowing in a more temperate environment, I set myself two more hours of effort before dinner, to take advantage of the cool weather and slightly reduced northeasterly winds that had dropped over the day.

Two hours later I was exhausted. It was almost 9 p.m. and Australia still looked close; the horizon was speckled with glowing yellow and orange lights. Most of the day I'd been eating home-made fruit cake, as it was quick and easy and I didn't want to stop rowing, so I was hungry and looking forward to my first freeze-dried meal. Digging deep into the storage compartments I pulled out a double-serve helping of beef and pasta hotpot, a flavour I hadn't tried. Next step was filling the cooker with water — I'd always assumed I could use salt water for cooking, but quickly realized this was not the case after my first mouthful of the world's saltiest beef and pasta hotpot. I forced myself to finish it, knowing that wasting food this early on would be tempting fate. Finishing my meal I experienced my first 'what do I do now?' moment. My two big fears were drifting back to shore overnight or drifting too far out to sea and into the path of a container ship. I also wanted to make sure I was taking advantage of any possible currents carrying me in the right direction. I sat on the deck for close to an hour pondering the best course of action. With no guide book to tell me or recommendation I could remember from anyone, I settled for climbing into the cabin, going to sleep and letting the boat drift, and waking myself every hour to check my position. I took a final glance around the darkness with the fear of container ships in the front of my mind before sliding into my cabin to prepare for my first night.

One of the electronic instruments I had on board was an automatic identification system (AIS) receiver called a WatchMate, which is a container-ship spotting device. Before I'd even unclipped my lifejacket from the safety rail, the WatchMate alarm sounded, indicating a container ship within 46 km, which is 25 nautical miles for those of you boaties reading this and used to the settings on a WatchMate. The ship was no concern as it was a whole 46 km away from me, but it was reassuring to see the alarm system was working perfectly. Knowing I'd have some warning if a ship was heading straight towards me was a weight off my mind.

The rest of the routine clicked into place. I called Michael and completed my first official check-in, letting him know I was feeling great and providing my position. Clouds sent me the weather text message, letting me know that the wind would blow me south and reach a maximum of 10 knots overnight. I turned the satellite phone off, wrapped it in a sealed plastic bag and locked it securely in a waterproof container. Steve's satellite phone was my precious link to the outside world and I would do everything I could to protect it on the voyage.

Lisa had put two bean bags in the cabin and I had a small self-inflating ground mattress, around 1.5 cm thick, which lay on top of the high-density foam covering the cabin floor. Certainly not the Hilton, but it would do and I arranged the bean bags around my upper body and head, ready to sleep. While I'd been on deck rowing the temperature was pleasant, with a slight sea breeze, but the cabin was steaming hot and humid — the roof was dripping with condensation after only 30 minutes. The cotton bean-bag covers were already starting to absorb the moisture in the air and I sat up to open the cabin door to try to vent the small space.

I felt like a piece of mouldy bread in a jar — not daring to sleep with the cabin door open and tempt being flooded so early in the trip. I tried to get used to the idea of sleeping in my own sweat, eventually getting nude and sitting up every 30 minutes or so to let air into the cabin.

Writing my name in the condensation on the roof, I realized I'd now spent close to two hours in the cabin and was still wondering what I should be doing. Utterly exhausted from the day's rowing, I was happy to see on my GPS screen that I was drifting south, which was no major concern, the WatchMate alarm hadn't been set off by any other ships and I was hoping that sooner or later I would be asleep.

I noticed the noise outside had increased and my radio antennas were whistling in the wind. I sat up as much as I could, my neck curled because of the low cabin roof, and undid the main cabin hatch to peer outside. The wind had certainly increased and the sea had begun to chop up into small white-capped waves popping up all around the boat and rocking *TTII* from side to side.

Relatively unconcerned by this I went back into my hovel of a cabin to think about the possible courses of action. As I was still struggling to work out the best method of dealing with the changing weather and toying with the idea of deploying the sea anchor, *TTII* was suddenly hit on the side of the cabin by what sounded like a bus, with the force throwing me against the opposite cabin wall. Slightly unsure about what had just happened, I moved my body back to balance the boat and paused, my feet pressed against the roof. Another wave rolled in and we repeated the manoeuvre. Slightly more prepared this time, I managed to lock myself into position with my feet and hands pressing up on the cabin roof. The small but steep waves had started breaking on *TTII*'s side and we were being blown side-on to the incoming waves, accentuating the rolling effect I was experiencing inside the cabin.

Holding myself still while I tried to think, I couldn't help feeling I was heading into something way out of my depth. These were only small waves and already I was being thrown around and wasn't sure how to deal with the situation. By now the boat was rocking violently, so much that I was constantly hitting either side of the cabin walls. It was now 2 a.m. and, unable to sleep, I wondered if I could do something to pull the bow of the boat into the oncoming waves without impeding the forward momentum that was the one positive thing about what the wind was doing.

I knew I had 40 m of rope in the front cabin, enough to swing the nose around if I threw it over the bow and attached it to the sea anchor bolts. Before venturing out on deck nude I reached

149

for my wet lifejacket just outside the front hatch to make sure I was tethered to *TTII* while crawling forward.

Cabin door locked behind me, I found the rope and tied it to the front bolt, hastily throwing the heavy rope over into the water. I closed the front hatch and scurried back into the cabin with the Tasman splashing me with one cold wave to say good night. Slowly, *TTII* swung around and began popping smoothly over most of the chop, nose first, with the drag of the rope providing just enough resistance to do the job.

Checking the time on my watch I saw that 4 a.m. had rolled around and I hadn't slept a wink. Anticipating what was coming next was keeping my heart rate up and sleep was clearly not going to be easy.

Rather than waking up to a 6 a.m. alarm I watched the numbers on my wristwatch tick over from 5.59, my finger poised to stop the alarm from beeping away. With a small sense of success after surviving my first night I began to wonder if every night would be the same, and how long I would survive with such limited sleep.

I peered through the hatch window. The weather looked good, with a clear blue sky. I stood up, half-in and half-out of the cabin door, to see the Australian coastline looking further away, by this stage appearing only a few millimetres above the horizon. With no ships in sight I reached forward and grabbed a couple of porridge bags.

Breakfast would be a combination of dried fruit and nuts mixed into a giant bowl of porridge, and of course a coffee, using fresh water this time. Hanging out for my first mouthful, I dipped my spoon into the bowl only to be hit by another wave, spilling half of my breakfast over my legs and all over the cabin floor. Tired and struggling not to lose my temper I tried to pretend nothing had happened and proceeded to eat my breakfast off the many different surfaces it now covered.

My next task was to go through what I liked to call my make-up routine, a process involving the application of a number of creams and lotions to prevent all the skin conditions I was likely to develop. First to be applied would be Sudocrem, more commonly used for babies' nappy rash. I put this lavishly over my entire backside and armpits, hoping to prevent chafing and pressure sores. Next on the agenda would be SPF 30+ sunblock on the back of my hands, face and feet. Because I rowed in a long-sleeved shirt and pants, I didn't need a full-body application and saved myself loads of time and sunblock. The most exciting part of what was to become a pretty tedious routine would be deciding which colour zinc to apply to my nose — fluorescent yellow, orange or blue.

Almost ready to start rowing, I put away the cooking equipment, washed my breakfast bowl in the sea and began to try to figure out which direction the wind was blowing in before making my second scheduled phone call to Michael. The wind seemed to be blowing from the north and had dropped a bit from early morning, reducing the number of steep, choppy waves. I took my satellite phone from its waterproof case, at the same time switching on my GPS system to confirm my coordinates.

It was great to hear his voice as I began the rehearsed check-in procedure by providing my GPS position and giving him the score for both my physical and mental well-being. Michael let me know I'd drifted around 28 km overnight, predominantly south, which I'd anticipated would happen over the first week. The East Australian Current was certainly working.

I was on the oars at around 8.15 a.m. and decided I would

have my first break at lunch time. Rowing *TTII* was heavy, with almost no momentum from each stroke. The night had been hard and long but my confidence grew as the day went on, and I was telling myself I could handle a far more severe hammering.

By the end of day two I had covered 54 km and was happy with my progress. The sun slowly dropped below the horizon, and with land still in sight I wondered if I would see Australia in the morning.

15 Quincey, meet Storm

As I went to sleep that night I knew I was in the middle of the coastal shipping lanes, with the possibility of a ship driving straight into me. I'd rowed for about 12 hours and at 10 p.m. had climbed into the cabin. Progress was good and I was sitting close to 37 km offshore. Clouds had warned me that the weather was taking a slight turn for the worse and the next few days would be slightly stormy, but on the lighter side the increase in wind would be coming from the west and helping push me home.

I decided to use the sea anchor and take advantage of the flowing current and the increasing westerly to get out of the shipping lanes as fast as possible. I checked on the GPS and, sure enough, I was drifting at about 1.2 knots towards the southwest, which meant I'd make some good overnight progress if I maintained my course.

My head had only been down for 20 minutes before my WatchMate alerted me to an approaching ship. Fortunately, the vessel was a long way off and of no concern. Moments later the alarm went off again, picking up another ship, this one heading a little closer towards me but still no real cause for worry. The WatchMate I was using had an option to either increase or decrease the search area. As the alarm continued to go off over the next few hours for ships that were

153

of no immediate danger, I decreased the search area on the WatchMate to 9.26 km (5 nautical miles), a distance I thought would make sure I wasn't woken up unnecessarily.

With the knowledge that the WatchMate was working effectively I was able to relax a bit, but the heat and condensation in the cabin combined with *TTII*'s rocking made it hard to get to sleep. At around 3 a.m. I was woken by the WatchMate alarm telling me a ship was travelling towards me at 22 knots and it weighed around 400 tons.

I threw open the cabin door and looked around but I couldn't see anything indicating ship's lights, nor could I hear an engine thrumming away. Taking another look at the GPS coordinates of the incoming vessel I pulled out my hand-held compass to figure out where the ship was in relation to *TTII*. Eventually, I tracked down a small light heading towards our stern. Over the next few minutes I stood on deck and watched as the vessel approached. Looking inside the cabin again to see where it was heading, I calculated that if I continued to move in the direction I was going, and if it also continued in the same direction, we would miss each other by about 2 km.

Not wanting to cause a fuss or receive unwanted attention, I kept quiet on the radio as I watched the gigantic shadow pass behind me, taking a moment to compare my 7-metre row boat with this eight-storey-high, 100-metre-long container ship, thinking how it would have made matchsticks out of me if it wasn't for the WatchMate.

I would be woken up again twice more that night, ensuring another crap sleep, but I would start the day with the fantastic surprise that I'd drifted nearly 56 km to the southeast overnight. The positive drift improved my mood and helped me deal with the sleep deprivation, and I managed to keep my breakfast in the bowl and get onto the oars fairly early. I had an unexpected fright at the lack of visible land. Australia was gone, another indication of progress in the right direction.

As I started to row I was surprised at how much better the boat was gliding compared with yesterday, with my boat speed reaching up to 4 knots. I had hit the East Australian Current, effectively doubling my speed towards New Zealand and making rowing much less of a battle. Excited at the prospect of making progress I got stuck into a solid three-hour block, covering 22 km.

During the morning row I noticed a shadow in the water, initially thinking it was my tired eyes playing tricks on me. As I continued to row, trying to stay in rhythm, the shadow appeared again, eventually gliding under the boat. I froze and didn't dare look over the edge. Momentarily gliding across the ocean surface, not wanting to break the water with my oars in case it attracted unnecessary attention, I waited patiently, watching the huge shape glide through the swells and eventually away from me. With no idea of what type of animal my visitor was, I had no interest in finding out. The fact that it was two metres wide was enough for me to row significantly harder for the next two hours to make sure I was well away from it.

After a solid morning of rowing and escaping from sea monsters the regime was taking its toll and my body was hurting fairly badly. I had stopped for lunch, which was enough time for my back to start stiffening up and make rowing awkward. This combined painfully with the development of two small blisters on my backside. I was being given an early lesson in pain management.

Clouds had warned me about approaching bad weather and

slowly the wind speed was building, along with the waves. Although I was making some good distance I was exhausted and started to feel incredibly depressed about what I was doing. As if something had just sucked the life out of me, over a period of 20 minutes I went from being positive and making good progress to having a complete breakdown, uselessly bursting into tears.

A small part of me was thinking, 'What on earth is going on? Why are you so upset?' The other 90 per cent of me had lost the plot. I absolutely hated what I was doing, it was incredibly hard and terrifying and I'd had enough. Distraught and confused I threw my oars inboard, climbed off the seat and sat at the back of the boat crying, thinking of ways I could give in and be picked up. For the life of me I couldn't figure out why the hell I'd decided to do this and sat sobbing for about an hour.

Slowly, I came to grips with things and climbed back up on my rowing seat. My next move could have been an easy call to the New South Wales police requesting a pick up. Completely and utterly over the trip, I sat there as rain slowly started to soak me through. I thought for a very long time about why I should continue, thinking mostly of the people who had helped me, trying to use that thought as motivation to pick up the blades and move on. I picked them up but started sobbing again, this time at the thought of being out there for an unknown amount of time. It was a strange situation. I'd dreamed about being here for years, but my dreams always involved finishing, not the mental and psychological battle I was now experiencing.

Something deep down started telling me I was never giving up, and the weird experience of dealing with thoughts screaming at me to stop and give in would now become my biggest battle.

After another hour or so of rowing I started to laugh at myself, calling myself a wimp and reminding myself to welcome the adventure and get on with enjoying the freedom. I'd made some good progress during my childlike sobbing — the good ole East Australian Current was pulling me southeast, and with me rowing 10 or more hours I ended up around 167 km away from land.

Calling Michael that night I didn't dare tell him about my emotional antics and went through the reporting routine. Slightly concerned about the approaching storm, we discussed some tactics and I settled in for the night. With the impending storm and high winds approaching I thought it would be wise to sleep in my wet-weather gear just in case I needed to get out on deck in a hurry. This wasn't a decision to be made lightly as it meant I would be ridiculously hot in the cabin and would certainly not sleep well.

Lying on my back dressed in my lifejacket and wet-weather gear, I looked around my cabin and was slightly disappointed with my interior decorating. I began to draw a picture of Mt Taranaki and next to it the coordinates for Taranaki, my proposed landing site. I then proceeded to write every single line of longitude and latitude I needed to pass through to reach New Zealand and would use these as a target and cross them off as I rowed through the various points. Cabin decorated, I applied another layer of Sudocrem to my backside to tackle a small itchy rash that was starting to appear and tried to get to sleep. It took about two hours to pass out and I was thankful for no more incoming ship alarms interrupting my sleep.

Despite the increasing wind and wave height I managed to get about two hours of solid sleep, and after the last two unsettled nights I definitely needed them. Checking my GPS coordinates sporadically overnight, I saw I was drifting at 3 knots, which was incredibly fast considering I wasn't rowing. Not wanting to slow down I decided to not use the sea anchor and take what I could to make some progress. No sea anchor meant *TTII* would probably rock around a lot more but she wouldn't be jerked over waves and wouldn't continuously throw me against the sides of the cabin during the night. Drifting and rolling, I would wake every 20 minutes to check the coordinates and see we were still making progress. I'd also check the deck to make sure all was well and everything was strapped in — by now the occasional wave was crashing over the side and flooding the deck.

Similar to turbulence on a plane, the violent rolls and twists were completely unpredictable and uncontrollable. I'd try to listen for an oncoming wave or when I was about to be hit, but failed to brace myself appropriately. Every single time I'd hit some part of my body against the wet fibreglass cabin walls. The Tasman was beginning to rear its ugly head and Clouds' predicted winds had arrived, blowing *TTII* swiftly across the lumpy surface.

I started moving my weight around the cabin in an attempt to counteract what was now extreme rocking — *TTII* was tipping from gunwale to gunwale with water washing over her deck. Wondering whether it was time for the sea anchor I looked at the GPS and we were now moving faster than ever in a southeasterly direction. I decided to let her go for it, the result being good progress but a sleepless and scary night.

Helplessly rolling around, I heard an incredible loud bubbling rumble for a few seconds before my body was launched up against the top corner of the cabin. I'd never ended up in this position before and briefly entertained the thought that perhaps I was upside down. At first glance I couldn't believe what I saw out the main cabin. We were on our side with water halfway up the hatch and a few trickles dribbling from the roof hatch vent. For a brief moment *TTII* was on her side, flipping back in seconds. I was mostly petrified but also chuffed that the boat I built took a big wave on her side and stayed afloat.

After popping my head out to check all my equipment was still on deck and latched on, I went back in the cabin and watched the clock tick over to 6 a.m., which meant it was time to start the day. The partial roll during the night was actually great, as it filled me with a new level of confidence about *TTII*'s ability to withstand a small amount of thrashing and right herself if overturned.

Still in my wet-weather gear, I ventured outside to make porridge, only to find that the sea was the most turbulent I'd seen so far. I climbed back into my cabin to make my scheduled phone calls and tell Michael about the roll and my current position.

Around 56 km of southeasterly progress overnight had made the partial capsize seem worthwhile but the situation outside was looking a bit ropey. I read through Clouds' weather report and saw his prediction that it would be too rough to row today. Stubborn as usual, I was convinced I'd be able to row. I went out on deck to give it a nudge and try to make some progress; after all, my only alternative was being thrown around all day in a stinking hot cabin.

As the boat rocked from side to side I pulled the oars out and carefully locked them into the rowlocks, watching out for rogue waves that could catch the blades and snap them in two. With my oars safely out I clipped on and took my first stroke. One oar blade buried itself completely while the other skimmed across the top of the water. My left arm jerked back suddenly with the lack of resistance. Gritting my teeth and sliding forward to take the next stroke the same thing happened. With only one oar loading up with water pressure and the other completely missing I wasn't going to get anywhere fast.

I decided I wouldn't give up trying until lunch time; with progress being made due to the wind and current I could at least try to take advantage by attempting to point the boat in the right direction with the oars. It didn't take long for frustration to set in, with me constantly missing strokes and *TTII* never level long enough to get a rhythm. I kept going and tried to line up a few waves to surf down for a bit of morning entertainment.

By now the increased winds had brought enormous ocean swells and the water below me was over 2000 m deep. This had the effect of reducing the steepness of the swells and they would roll smoothly under *TTII* with the odd gust of wind dumping the top of the occasional one onto me. I was in awe of the size of these swells and floating to the top of one I looked back over the boat and saw hundreds upon hundreds lined up, some smooth and some chopped up by the winds. I was struggling to comprehend the vastness of the playground I was in.

It was lunch time and rowing was pointless. Checking on the GPS, I could see that all my efforts didn't seem to either decrease or increase my speed so I began to pack up my oars and decided to have lunch before heading into the cabin.

At this stage I battled with every decision, trying to make the absolute correct one to ensure the most progress was made, knowing that the inevitable consequence of a bad decision would mean less progress, or even worse, I would go backwards.

Lunch was good and I slipped into the cabin, my clothing soaked. I tried to get nude without getting water everywhere.

Brother Ben looking after Shaun.

RIGHT: Shaun with brothers Ben (left) and David (right).

BELOW LEFT: A very cool dude, at Narrow Neck Beach, North Shore.

BELOW RIGHT: Dad Colin, mum Nannette, Shaun and Ben.

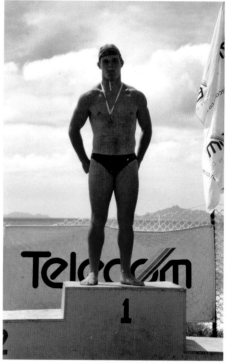

TOP LEFT: With mum Nannette.

ABOVE: At Waipu Cove, standing tall.

LEFT: Marcus Beach, Queensland, Australia.

Shaun and his dad on Marcus Beach in Queensland. New Zealand is in that direction!

Dad Colin rowing out of Hokianga Harbour in 1977.

Tasman Trespasser II on the first day of construction at Salthouse Boatbuilders, the same place *TTI* was built in 1977.

Construction continues.

The keel and hull completed, *TTII* is flipped over.

The bow of *TTII* was tricky as it needed to be incredibly strong to hold the sea anchor.

The cabin being built, with Dave Yallop the boat builder in deep concentration.

With assistance from the Salthouse engineers, the instrument rack is attached.

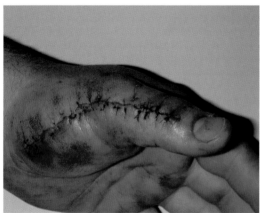

ABOVE: Painted and almost ready.

LEFT: One slip with a chisel and 28 stitches later.

BELOW: *TTII*'s first outing down to Mairangi Bay beach on Auckland's North Shore.

Orcon Internet and Timex Watches branding is added to the paintwork.

With signwriting completed by Cube Creative Print, Design & Signage, *TTII* was now ready to go.

TTII launch on Takapuna Beach. Shaun and Lisa couldn't break the bottle, so they decided to spray it instead.

Testing *TTII* without a rudder.

New Zealand Geographic

Training in *TTII* on Hauraki Gulf.

More training on the Hauraki Gulf.

Team Tasman at Coffs Harbour on the first night that everybody arrived to prepare *TTII* for her voyage. From left, Jill Jones, Winton Jones, Oliver Young, Shaun, Lisa Jones and Michael Buck.

Rodger Badham and Shaun review the incoming weather reports and decide to delay the departure date by a few days. From left, Colin Quincey, Oliver Young, Rodger Badham, Winton Jones and Shaun.

Little boat surrounded by big cliffs. Training in Coffs Harbour, Australia.

The day of departure and Lisa helps pack the boat.

Finally making some progress.

The first sunset out on the Tasman.

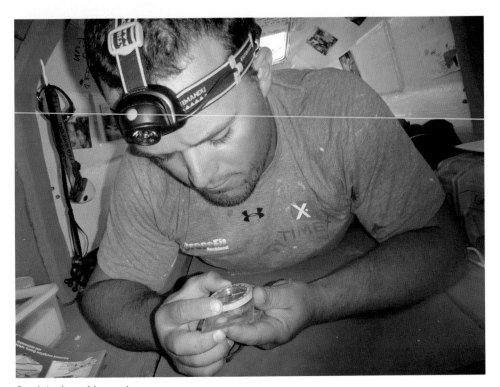

Stuck in the cabin, again.

A storm is brewing.

On this particular day it was almost impossible to see because of the intense sea spray.

Shaun woke up every day to these words. It was all about believing.

Blisters, which after a few days peeled back to raw skin.

Snapped
sea anchor
attachment
point.

One of the few
calm days.

Trying to dry all
the equipment.

Shaun wearing his crucial sunglasses, which he lost when he capsized.

The one and only washing day.

Concerned about whether my decision to stop rowing was the right one, I was irritated at the thought that I had given up too easily. After all, it was only the fourth day and already I'd let conditions stop me rowing.

Rolling around in the cabin I watched the GPS numbers slowly change while the ocean splashed over the bow and onto the cabin window. At night I could manage being in the cabin as there was a purpose involved — sleeping. But during the day I would grow increasingly inpatient and confused as I played mind games around what I ought to be doing.

Should I attempt to row or should I rest in the stinky cesspool cabin? Putting the sea anchor out and getting thrown around on the same spot and waiting it out was an absolute nightmare for me and I would always want to be doing something to assist the situation. Thankfully, I would only be in the cabin until the next morning. The wind had slowly dropped overnight, providing a slightly better night's sleep and another fantastic drift towards New Zealand. I'd had another terrible night but progress had been made and I was now roughly 333 km off the coast of Australia.

It was the morning of my fifth day and I was proud of myself and ready to take on the Tasman again. The waves were still about and only the odd cheeky one would splash over the boat, still tipping my world from side to side but letting me sit from time to time.

Preparing meals involved boiling or heating close to a litre of fresh water in my JetBoil, a type of gas cooker that could boil water from cold within one minute. Due to the constant rocking I would have to hold the cooker while it boiled. This particular morning I was sitting in my usual outdoor position, with a bowl of dry porridge and nuts in one hand and the JetBoil heating

161

away in the other, trying not to let the salt-water spray mix in with the dry food.

Just as the water was almost boiled the boat jerked unpredictably and I spilled the dry food all over myself and dropped the JetBoil cooker onto my foot. This resulted in a significant amount of gas shooting out of the butane canister and covering my bare legs in an interesting mixture of flames and hot water from the cooker. Jumping backwards in panic I kicked the canister again, releasing another squirt of gas and more flame. I looked down to see my legs had all the hairs burnt off, but seemed to be fine otherwise.

Reaching into the foot well to turn the gas off I cursed myself for being foolish and much too complacent, causing a potentially expedition-ending accident. Luckily, I'd come off without any injuries, just slightly frightened and angry at myself for being such a bloody idiot. I was upset for some time before starting to think about rowing.

But the bad start to the day was only a small indication of what was to come. After only three hours of frustrating rowing before lunch time I was ready to pack it in again, thanks to my recently charred legs.

Due to the rough conditions over the past few days I'd decided that washing was a low priority and I'd started to develop a very itchy rash over my back and thighs. Waiting in the cabin for time to pass, my mind very quickly wanted to focus on the itchy rash, so I spent close to an hour wiping my body with a cloth dampened with fresh water before applying loads of Sudocrem to the affected areas. The itch factor reduced ever so slightly. Small waves continued to hit *TTII* and I watched time roll past as the light outside slowly turned to dark as I tried not to think very hard about anything. Another night was coming and I couldn't help but feel as if I'd spent more time in my cabin waiting to be able to row than I had actually rowing towards New Zealand.

I was waiting for Clouds' next weather text. As the satellite phone beeped away, I read the following:

new [computer] models have NE-E-ESE/30–40 for 4–6 days from FRI.
Nasty low 2 Nth, high 2 Sth
Be good 2 be 34–35S for current by then

I was so tired it didn't take much to break me and this message certainly did. From Friday I was going to be hit with a six-day storm, blowing me back towards Australia. Until now my time in the cabin had been coupled with positive drift and wind direction, which took the edge off my frustration at not being able to row. I had two days' countdown until the storm would hit and I'd have to row incredibly hard to reach the best possible position to take on the beast of a storm that was brewing.

Just hearing the voices at home that night when I made my scheduled calls was enough to depress me into hanging up a number of times, pretending it was bad reception while I collected myself to start talking again.

I forced myself to try to sleep, knowing that the next two days would be full steam ahead rowing. I'd set my alarm an hour early, getting out of the cabin quickly and trying not to dwell on the weather forecast from the night before.

An amazing sunrise greeted me, followed by a whale's tail lifting up into the air about a kilometre away before it dived into the deep. A brilliant morning. I was set to tick off a few kilometres and hopefully get into a good position for the approaching storm. The next few hours I watched as the weather became increasingly overcast, with thick, angry clouds forming behind me. It wasn't long before the sky was a collection of dark, grey, gigantic clouds. The sea was only slightly lumpy and I was rowing along well at about 3 knots when I was almost frightened off my rowing seat by an almighty boom from the clouds above. The thunderous roar was incredible, followed by an equally impressive lightning bolt igniting the sky. A magnificent display of nature's light and sound and I had a front row seat (ha ha) feeling more than ever at nature's mercy as the booms from above slightly rattled me.

At first this was great to watch, until I noticed the ocean had become smooth and I was by far the highest point above the water, especially with my 2 m radio aerials. I'd never even considered lightning-strike as a risk but the result of one would be devastating. I stood up to detach my radio aerials, watching as a number of lightning bolts in the distance grounded themselves on the surface. With the aerials down I thought about what I could do to reduce the risk of lightning-strike. I collected all the spare stainless wire I had around the boat and attached to *TTII*'s high points, trailing the wires into the water. My theory was that if we were struck, hopefully the majority of the charge would flow through the wire and into the ground before electrocuting me in my cabin. I continued happily rowing through the lightning storm, only considering in hindsight that while I was rowing my head was now the highest point on the boat.

The thunder and lightning increased into the night. Sleeping was hard enough without the boat jerking and rolling from side to side. I had decided to use the sea anchor this evening to get the most value out of the southeasterly flowing current. With the sea anchor jerking the boat around and the thunder blasting I felt as if I'd been tossed into a battlefield and was trying my best to sleep through it. Terrified of being fried in my cabin by a lightning strike, I stayed awake watching the sky light up with consistent flashes.

Desperately grasping at the positive side of things, I reminded myself I'd spent my first week on the Tasman and made some 480 km of progress towards New Zealand and so far I hadn't been either sunk or fried. Nevertheless, I couldn't help but fear the easterly storm that was now rapidly approaching. Not really sure how best to prepare for it, I stuck to the routine I had started to develop and just rowed as hard as I could to get myself to the position Clouds had suggested would be the best to ride out the storm.

16 Worst 10 days of my life

I had survived a lightning storm and managed to make some solid progress, but the easterly storm was approaching and today was my last day to try to hit a particular point deemed the best place to ride out the bad weather.

The dark clouds had moved on and I had started rowing early, slightly panicked by the thought of easterly winds approaching at any moment. I would take advantage of the calm water and row as long and hard as I could, so from 7.30 a.m. till 12.30 p.m. I rowed without a break. This was the longest session I'd completed so far and, chuffed with my efforts, I whipped up a fast meal consisting of a Mars bar and freeze-dried spaghetti Bolognaise.

Sucking the food down as quickly as I could to get on with rowing, I glanced over the side to start washing my food bowl and saw I had a couple of visitors. Two little black and white fish were darting around underneath me and watching them kept me entertained for a few moments as they both went crazy over my food scraps. The fish were the first of my unique visitors that day, as a moth of some sort glided his way onto the main cabin door. I couldn't help but laugh thinking about how happy that moth must have been to see me, some 500 km away from land. The moth disappeared about as quickly as he arrived, but Mother Nature was doing her best to keep me company that day. I was also treated to some small seabirds swooping and skimming their wings along the top of the water. Watching them immediately took my mind away from rowing and I'd find myself happily watching away as time disappeared faster than normal. Progress was slow. A quick check of the GPS and I realized that at my current speed I wasn't going to reach the coordinates I was targeting. I tried rowing harder and expending more energy but this wasn't sustainable. I needed to be lighter and I started to think about unnecessary equipment or supplies.

Rummaging through the boat numerous items started to disappear overboard, the first to go was a 3 kg power inverter, which I was going to use to charge my laptop. Next was 14 kilos of lead ballast, weight I would replace with salt water once it was needed. Numerous other items, including books and clothing, all went to Davy Jones's locker. Sometime during this process I regretfully also threw out my toothbrush. (Don't ask — I know it makes no sense now. You had to be there.)

I jumped on the oars again to see if I had made any noticeable difference and we glided through the water more smoothly and 0.3 of a knot faster. Dumping the weight in hindsight may not have helped a huge amount in terms of boat speed, but mentally I needed to know I wasn't hauling anything extra and was as efficient as possible. Settled in my head that I was now efficient, I rowed with a couple of water breaks until it was time to call Michael.

Michael had spoken to Clouds about the incoming weather patterns, concerned that I wasn't going to reach the way point. We decided together that I would row through the night until I either reached the coordinates or the weather turned against me. Straight back on the oars after dinner I put extra foam padding on my seat. Some painful sores were starting to develop and I needed to be able to focus on the rowing. The sun had disappeared and I glided through the dusk, a bit excited to be night rowing but also nervous about what it might entail. The sun was replaced by moonlight glistening on water that looked like reflective tin foil, with each oar stroke sparking a small pool of phosphorescence on the surface.

Nearing 11 p.m. I started to develop tunnel-like vision towards my glowing white GPS unit, watching each number tick over as I slowly approached the magic coordinates. Nothing else in the world mattered, as stroke by stroke I drew nearer. *TTII* and I were moving as a unit and for the first time the water was calm enough for me to develop a distinct rhythm with the same sounds repeating themselves at different points of the stroke. I was certainly in the zone and didn't want to stop.

Midnight was approaching and checking my watch I saw I'd now been rowing for a total of 15 hours and was only half a mile away from where I needed to be. A few hundred metres away from the point my eyes welled up and on hitting the mark I threw out a controlled air punch, claiming my victory, then slid off my seat to lie on the deck. In a mix of tears and laughter I rigged the parachute anchor in anticipation of the easterly winds and threw it overboard. After hauling in the oars I moved slowly into the cabin, carrying a happy little grin to bed.

Lying down it hit me how tired I was and because the ocean was smooth I was looking forward to a relatively good night's sleep. Waking every hour or so I noticed I was moving in a positive easterly direction, and between 1 a.m. and 3 a.m. clocked up a few extra kilometres towards New Zealand. Sadly, this came to an abrupt halt somewhere between 3 a.m. and 4 a.m. when an easterly breeze started to build and sudden little jerks on the sea anchor started to happen.

That morning, still positive about the day before, I told Michael I needed to take the good with the bad and that I'd try rowing into the wind today to reduce any westerly drift. I hit the oars at about 8 a.m. after some extra sleep to recover from the massive day before and then brought in the sea anchor.

The easterlies had started and I was rowing into some light winds, with *TTII* moving at an impressively slow 0.1 knots towards New Zealand. Trying not to think about the futility of the situation, I tried to convince myself it was worth the hard slog. I figured any progress was good and I would do everything I could to slow my drift back to Australia while I could still row safely in the conditions.

The most challenging aspect of rowing into the wind was the way *TTII* would be blown off course as the wind caught the side of the boat and pushed her, immediately requiring about 10 hard strokes on one arm spinning on the spot and killing all our boat speed. I would then row 10 strong strokes with both arms to gain some momentum to try to maintain a course, with only the briefest lapse of concentration spinning the boat again, which meant having to repeat the exercise. It was a fruitless battle that would go on till lunch time, eventually defeating me as the wind stepped up a notch and I was now heading back towards Australia.

Wake up, put wet-weather clothing on, eat food, cover face in sunblock and cover bum in Sudocrem (in that order) then get on the oars as soon as possible to avoid depressing thought process. Repeat the last four steps for lunch and dinner and sleep when tired.

If I swayed in any way from that routine I would find myself bitterly depressed and would struggle to summon the motivation to get out of the cabin and start rowing. Strict adhesion to routine was the key to each day and the incoming easterly storm would play havoc with my ability to develop one, effectively taking away everything I could control.

Moving quickly to rig the sea anchor, I had already drifted back further than I had rowed over the past four hours and slowing this backwards drift became my number-one priority. Slowly I released the sea anchor and watched it expand and fill with water. When it was full it began to pull out the rope and retrieval line faster than it had before, catching me off guard as it tangled around my feet. I stepped out of the loops and managed to get control of the nylon rope, feeding it out over the bow. As the sea anchor line was pulled tight I was knocked backwards. I found this strange, as previously the uptake of tension on the line had been far more gradual. I made my way to the back of the *TTII*, slightly curious.

Watching the GPS I noticed we had immediately started to move towards New Zealand again at a rate of 0.7 knots, which was six times as fast as when I was rowing. A little bitter at this I decided to call Clouds to get his interpretation of the various currents in the area.

Clouds happily informed me that due to the extra ground I'd covered overnight I was at the top of a gigantic clockwise-moving eddy, which meant the water just under the surface was moving towards New Zealand while the water on the surface was being blown towards Australia. The only problem for me was that with the current moving against the wind direction, it increased the steepness of the waves flowing towards me. As the wind continued to blow, the size of the waves increased. I sat at the back of the boat revelling in the fact that my sea anchor was slowly dragging me along and I was beating the wind. It was obvious I would be unable to row in these conditions, as I could barely hold on just sitting there. I was completely soaked and thoroughly enjoying the waves crashing over the nose of the boat, so I decided to kill some time with the hand-fishing line I'd brought with me.

Opening the packet of artificial soft baits I began lowering the line with solid expectations of landing something decent. With no bites in the first 10 minutes I lowered the line deeper and played around with different depths for a good hour or so. Absolutely nothing seemed to be interested in my bait and as the wave height began to increase I decided to pull in the fishing line and start preparing to get into the cabin.

I knew the weather was going to get increasingly bad over the next few days and I could possibly be in the cabin for quite some time, so thinking ahead I took two day-packs of food in with me just in case, and a few bottles of water.

As I had put one leg into the cabin I crouched down to slide my body in at the exact same time as a wave hit the boat and lurched it to one side. The inside edge of the cabin door hit me in the side of the my jaw, knocking me onto the floor, closely followed by a spray of water covering the cabin floor. Slightly dazed, I turned quickly to close the door before checking my jaw. My face would be bruised but was thankfully intact. I left my wet jacket and pants on, not knowing when I would need to launch out of the cabin to fix something.

Very slowly we were heading towards New Zealand. It was

171

now close to 5 p.m. and I had spent most of the day outside, either fishing or rowing. The wind was certainly starting to howl and the waves were beginning to crash like never before. It was clearly going to be a hard night. I braced my mind and body for the long haul.

With no good news to report in the morning, Michael informed me I'd begun to move around the far right side of the giant eddy, slowly moving me southwest, which confirmed my early morning calculations. Clouds' weather report came through and I received three messages: the first informed me that conditions were worse than he thought and I could expect no rowing for up to six days, the next told me I was in a current moving back towards Sydney and the last text message told me I was about to begin to understand what my father had gone through. Throughout the night I'd been thrown around a bit and hadn't slept, so the text message ripped away any ounce of positivity I had left. Frozen like a stunned mullet, I sobbed and wondered how on earth I was going to get through the next week.

Looking out the window, all I could see were deep blue waves, hundreds upon hundreds, rolling towards me from the east, each blue bastard eating at my patience and willingness to persevere. A single wave would rock the boat from side to side at least seven or eight times, each time to the gunwales, and just as it was about to stop another wave would come. The violent rocking was something I would never get used to, every second or third wave crashed over the nose or side-splashed the cabin door, filling the cockpit and making exiting the cabin treacherous.

I opened the cabin door only a millimetre to let some air

in, only to be splashed as yet more water came inside the already sweat-soaked cabin. Frustrated at *TTII*'s repertoire of unpredictable movements, my only option was to lie on my back in full wet-weather gear, with condensation dripping off the roof and sweat off my forehead slowly seeping down the arms of my jacket and trousers. My legs are up in the air braced against the roof, as in my mind I'm mentally preparing and planning constantly for the worst, putting all my faith in the sea anchor holding me head-on into the oncoming barrage.

As I was thrown around inside the cabin I tried to keep myself entertained by either navigating or listening to music. Everything else seemed impossible due to the consistent turbulence. I didn't bother trying to prepare food and didn't feel as if I needed any, as I wasn't rowing or really expending any energy moving around for that matter. All movement was courtesy of the Tasman.

Hour upon hour I was trapped in the steamy cabin waiting for time to hurry up so I could get on with my adventure. A few times I caught myself swearing at the Tasman, then quickly reneging on my comments as I tried not to look at the water as having some sort of personality. But the sleep deprivation and frustration built up slowly and I eventually completely lost my temper at the Tasman Sea, using the foulest words I knew. Telling myself if was just a sea, with no personality or soul, and that what was happening was merely a combination of environmental factors which would soon pass and I could continue, did no good at all. I hated the bastard.

As night rolled around I'd been in the cabin for about 30 hours and I cheered up a bit at the thought that if I went to sleep a whole bunch of hours would pass while I was otherwise occupied.

Tonight my world would be another collection of violent twists, rolls and thuds combined with the noise of howling wind and waves crashing into, onto and over me. I'd had enough. I knew I had a strong mind but I had to really remind myself that it was just a matter of time until it was my turn to make progress. Fighting it will do nothing, rowing against it will do nothing — I was officially redundant and I would have to wait for the invincible bully to drop its guard.

Somehow I survived the night with my sanity intact, watching as the darkness outside slowly turned into daylight. The conditions had worsened and I was facing another day in my cesspool of a cabin, with no breakfast and only my epilepsy medication and a multivitamin to start the day. I stayed on my back trying to anticipate the next wave.

Two more days would pass this way as the easterly storm raged. By now partially crippled by the mind games I was playing, I was seriously thinking about giving up or rowing back when *TTII* spun around in a strange direction, floating broadside to the oncoming waves.

This was very bad, as it meant the waves would now dump straight onto the side of the boat, potentially rolling *TTII* down the face of the wave, and we were now drifting twice as fast towards Australia. Trying to work out what had happened I looked out the cabin window to see the face of a wave about to dump on our side. Trying to counteract the wave I moved to the oncoming side of the cabin, potentially avoiding a full roll. The impact was massive, sucking part of the boat under and submerging the cockpit. Fortunately, I was well positioned and stayed locked in place. Once the water had receded from the deck I decided I needed to get outside and figure out what was wrong with the sea anchor. I threw on my wet-weather jacket and decided to leave my pants off to avoid them getting wet. I had my lifejacket on and I paused, anticipating the best moment to get outside and clip onto the safety wire.

A small wave crashed over the side and before the next one arrived I jumped out and clipped on, closing and locking the cabin door behind me. I scrambled up to the bow and with just enough time to brace for impact I crouched below the front edge of the bow storage compartment to avoid a splash in the face, before hanging over the edge to see what was happening. The bolt used to fasten the sea anchor to *TTII* had sheared in half, ripping out a chunk of wood. My first thought was to check whether we were leaking, so I opened the bow compartment and was relieved to see it was still watertight.

In mounting panic I noticed the retrieval line used to collapse and haul the parachute anchor in was still attached to a cleat on top of the bow compartment. An exploratory pull on the line told me there was a significant amount of drag. I started to pull the line in. It was incredibly heavy. Hoping desperately that the sea anchor was still attached I continued to pull. With each wave that crashed over the bow *TTII* would be sucked down the front of the wave and all the line I had just pulled in would be pulled straight back out again. Most of the time I was able to at least pull on the line, and this kept *TTII* nose-on into the waves, but on the odd occasion there was nothing I could do and I would be washed down the deck.

After an hour and a half of struggling with the line, I finally hauled the sea anchor to the boat's edge and I lifted it up out of the water to find the other half of the steel bolt still attached.

I couldn't believe the bolt had snapped. I clearly remember discussing this exact scenario with the guy who sold it to me, and I knew it had a 6-ton breaking strain. I was sure that level of force hadn't been applied. The sea anchor was a complete bird's nest and I began to untangle the shambles, sometimes cutting the rope to speed up the process.

The untangling and redeployment would take me another hour and I would be washed around the deck a number of times. Utterly exhausted by now, I made my way back to the cabin hoping to finally get some rest. While the sea anchor was out of the water I had lost 17 km of progress, added to the 232 km I'd already lost over the past four days.

As I braced myself in the cabin after removing the wet-weather gear, my lower back instantly started to scream at me. I had obviously pulled a muscle bringing in the broken sea anchor. Thankful for once that I wasn't rowing, I took a few painkillers and an anti-inflammatory pill and tried to avoid using my back as I started waiting. Again.

It was Sunday, two days after the sea-anchor incident, and I had now spent seven days in my cabin waiting for the storm to recede. Clouds had predicted that the storm would ease on Monday but that still didn't guarantee row-able conditions. I had filled the days with watching the clock and playing mind games about how long I thought it was going to take. Speaking to friends and family just upset me and at times life only seemed manageable if I focused solely on the next 10 minutes.

After eight days of cabin life I looked outside to see what looked like a semi-reasonable day, with no waves spilling over into the cockpit. I slowly sat up and started to open the cabin door. By now I'd spent the same amount of time in my cabin as I had rowing, and in a weird way the outside was just as unfamiliar and daunting as the inside had been. Institutionalized by cabin lifestyle I closed the door again to pick up the satellite phone and find out what the weather was doing.

I had been too scared to check the weather forecast over the previous couple of days as the storm increased, so I decided to call Clouds and find out what the story was. He said things were looking better and I would definitely be rowing over the next few days. Although this was great news I struggled to get excited. In fact I couldn't get enthusiastic about anything. I just didn't care any more. Over the past eight days I had travelled in a massive loop with the circling currents and was in the exact same place I had been nine days ago.

It looked as if I had to completely rebuild my psychological outlook in order to start attacking the Tasman all over again. Eight days cooped up in the small tube I called a cabin had ruined my usual enthusiastic and positive outlook. On the morning of day nine I called Lisa, as I did every day, and found myself telling her I couldn't get up and start rowing. I had developed a mind block that wouldn't allow me to get out through the door and get on with it. She listened patiently to my ramblings and as she gently talked to me I started to change the way I was thinking. I had now wasted three hours lying in the cabin waiting for an injection of enthusiasm, of which there was absolutely none. I eventually and painfully convinced myself that the fastest way out of the situation was to change how I was looking at it. I started to tell myself off for not being grateful about the unique position I was in and how lucky I was

177

to still be alive, let alone still able to row. As I kept focusing on the different aspects of my little world I had to be grateful for, I slowly found some enthusiasm and made my way out of the cave of depression.

By now I was outside, amazed at how quickly the negative feelings had disappeared. I knew they were still hanging about somewhere in my head but I now had a way to deal with them and I would certainly start to focus on all the cool things about my funny little ocean-rowing world.

Climbing on the oars, I still had to dig very deep, rowing with almost no progress as the residual swell from the past eight days of easterlies continued pushing me back. I had overcome a massive hurdle and *TTII* had taken on and survived a substantial storm. Now I had developed a relentless determination to get home as fast as possible. Having been at sea for 22 days I would make my next focus hitting the halfway mark of 163 degrees of longitude.

17 Two steps forward, one-and-a-half back

With seven days trapped in the cabin behind me, I took forward the attitude that life couldn't possibly get much worse. While this was tempting fate, I had to hold on to something to stay positive.

Now more than ever I eagerly waited for Clouds' weather text, which would act as a complete barometer to my mood for the day. When Clouds predicted strong westerly winds my smile grew from ear to ear as I hurried around the boat trying to get on the oars as soon as possible.

With the increased westerly winds approaching I had to do everything I could to make *TTII* move as fast as possible through the water. This would lead me to start thinking about climbing into the water to scrub the bottom of her hull. Thinking for a very long time about the prospect of swimming in the shark-infested waters 700 km off the coast of Australia, it took me an even longer time to contemplate having a look over the side to see if the boat was dirty. As I rummaged through the storage compartments looking for my mask and paint scraper, I was reminded of a conversation I'd had with Roy from the boat-building yard at Coffs, about how important it was to use anti-fouling paint on the bottom of the boat.

I spent about five minutes searching the surface for fins or for anything that would or could possibly bite or chew on me before dunking my head over the side to check out the hull. The surface was all clear with no biters in sight and I put my head in to see close to an inch of growth over the entire hull. Thousands of alien-like small creatures wearing green fur had decided my hull was the best place to be. The worst part about it was that I would now need to climb overboard and spend a long time in the water scraping and scrubbing until she was clean.

Building up to the big plunge I paced up and down the boat, thinking through what I was about to do, initially thinking I should reduce the amount of time I spent in the water by scrubbing as much as I could from the edge of the boat. Dangling half-in and half-out of the 4000-m-deep Tasman, I began to scrape away at the small ecosystem responsible for slowing my progress home, managing to only chip off a small amount before realizing it was time for the inevitable.

Taking a bit more time to contemplate the splash, I grabbed my underwater camera with the idea of filming underneath the boat for a few minutes and then looking at the footage. If there were any sharks I wouldn't get in. The footage showed nothing but a very dirty boat, which meant I was going for a dip. In another half-in, half-out scrubbing attempt, I would very ungracefully slip out of the boat, making an almighty splash, only to immediately clamber back in, thinking I'd just attracted all the sharks in the Tasman.

Repeating the process, I found myself floating in beautifully clear water, scraping away at the hull between deep breaths. The first 15 minutes in the water I was incredibly nervous, constantly looking over my shoulder every few seconds while halfheartedly cleaning the hull. I soon realized being in the water was absolutely amazing. Not only was the water the clearest spectrum of clean blue colour, but more importantly, my entire world stopped rocking and for the first time in 23 days I was sitting still, just floating in the water.

I would spend a good hour in the water cleaning the boat meticulously, ensuring every single barnacle was removed, thinking each one had the ability to slow me down on my way home.

As I hit the oars again I was amazed at the increase in speed of up to 1.8 knots, and at the same time very annoyed that I hadn't cleaned the hull earlier. I was making some great speed and as the westerly winds started to increase I was making my best progress so far, clearing 93 km in a day of rowing, which was almost an entire degree of longitude. New Zealand didn't seem quite so far away.

I reported in to Michael, letting him know about my great day, closely followed by Clouds' text message saying more westerly winds were on the way. With no sea anchor out I was excited about getting a good night's sleep with a good chance of making progress. Over the past 10 days I'd become used to waking up each morning closer to Australia, so this was exciting.

Knowing that the weather was slightly more stable and we were heading in the right direction, I managed a few solid two-hour blocks of sleep, which felt brilliant after what I'd been through. With no time to waste I breezed through the morning routine, wanting to hit the oars as soon as possible to take advantage of the following seas. Looking at the GPS, I could see that even when I wasn't rowing we were still heading in the right direction at 2 knots, which made me want to row hard even more.

The following conditions, combined with my rowing, meant I was recording speeds of up to 7 knots and even surfing down waves — absolutely exhilarating compared with my normal routine. As the day flew by suddenly it was lunch time and I'd clocked up a never-before-seen 37 km, making my average speed for the morning around 4 knots.

Lunch was a hurried affair, as I was thinking that if I worked hard I might be able to break Dad's record of 111 km in one day. The wind was blowing and the bumpy sea was moving in the right direction, just before *TTII* suddenly bumped into something and the bow starting lifting out of the water.

The boat's sudden halt gave me a surprise, which was nothing compared to the shock I got once I stood up to look around and see what the story was. As I peered over the bow a smooth silvery head the size of a small van broke through the surface, with the remainder of its massive body visible under the bow. I felt all the blood rush out of my face as the whale's square head was now higher out of the water than the top of my boat and I jumped to the safety line running the length of the boat, wrapping my arms around it, convinced the whale would roll or hit the boat again.

I waited two or three minutes before looking over the side to see the full length of the sperm whale about 100 m away, with the length of its back now showing above water. With my heart thumping at around 180 beats per minute I was on the oars and getting away as fast as I could, not wanting to tempt the massive animal's curiosity.

After a solid hour of rowing I burst out laughing at the complete and absolute uniqueness of what had just happened, thinking I must be part of a very small group of people who have rowed into a sperm whale's head.

After reporting the incident to Michael I needed to focus again on the rowing as progress was still ticking over phenomenally well and Dad's record was in reach. With my mind fully focused on the whale incident I wasn't as preoccupied with the time and it went past very quickly. Unfortunately, the wind dropped and my speed was almost cut in half, saving Dad's record for another day.

I was in the cabin by 9 p.m. getting ready to try to sleep, but the weather report wasn't the best, with 10 hours of easterly winds predicted for the next day. I decided I would continue rowing until midnight, before rigging the sea anchor and preparing for a day in the cabin. Reluctant to stay in the cabin all day I set my alarm an hour early to try to catch the smooth early morning conditions before the easterly picked up.

Having made only a few kilometres over three hours I hauled the oars in, tied them down and reset the sea anchor before settling in for another long, boring day in the cabin. The sea wasn't big or stormy but it was still strong enough to ensure no progress towards New Zealand. I ended up spending the whole day in the cabin thinking about the whale incident, laughing at how much more of a fright the whale would have had. I lost around 33 km over 10 hours of easterly winds, which was frustrating but definitely not as bad as I had experienced in the past and good weather was on its way.

That night wasn't pleasant with only a few hours of sleep, and sometime during the night the wind changed, swinging around to the north and eventually to the northwest, slowly blowing me back on track for the halfway mark. There was only a small amount of westerly in the wind and the ocean was extraordinarily choppy and I watched as 2 m waves crashed into each other, shooting water directly up into the air. A very strange phenomenon, I thought, surely they're meant to flow in the same direction? I found myself being pushed and rolled in all sorts of directions and making absolutely no progress. I'd never seen the sea looking like this and it was behaving in a very strange way.

Slightly nervous by now, I called Clouds and asked him to take a look at what was going on. It took him a few hours to figure it out, eventually telling me I was on the edge of an underwater mountain which was dramatically increasing the current flowing from the southeast to the northwest, and I was attempting to row directly into it. I was given the same advice as I was for most of the expedition and that was to row as hard and as long as I could towards New Zealand and eventually break from the current.

I could easily have given up rowing for the day, but with the thought of drifting back towards Australia overnight pushing me to get back on the oars I rowed for 10 hours at 0.2 knots, eventually pulling free of the increased currents and we were heading towards New Zealand again.

Day 27 on the Tasman, and I had now experienced three days of rain and been surprised at how it affected my mood. I woke up and peered out the cabin door, which was like looking out the windscreen of a car driving through a stormy night at 100 kph, and as I stepped out to start my day, it felt fairly similar.

With the first few days of rain I was quite excited, as Dad had described in his book a time when the rain was so heavy it looked as though it bounced off the surface, describing the water as looking like a never-ending shag-pile carpet. Curious about what this looked like, I was happy to match the description with the reality, but the rain washed away my small moment of reflection and I very quickly started to get sick of everything being wet. The rain finally stopped at 2 p.m. the next day, and instead the sun poured down on me, disappearing a few times behind the odd dark cloud.

My mood quickly improved. The day also brought some fairly sizeable waves rolling in from the west and I was given my first opportunity to start really surfing *TTII*. Surfing a wave in the right direction was the ultimate feeling of satisfaction, as it was a combination of progress and pure adrenaline-pumping fun. The swell grew higher and steeper and I cleared the decks and locked everything in the cabins, preparing to surf some large swells as I rowed towards New Zealand.

On the first wave I tried I gave a few massive strokes to increase my speed and just missed it. Next time I started putting the big strokes in a bit earlier and, bingo, I was shooting down at 8 knots, which at this time was my highest recorded speed. I kept trying to catch waves but was missing more than I was catching and decided to move more weight to the front of the boat to increase my luck.

I moved about 30 kilos of water into the front compartments and sure enough I was catching almost every wave, even when I wasn't rowing. It was a bit crazy at times, even eating lunch while shooting down the front of a wave.

A gigantic green wave was building a few hundred metres behind me and I had to decide to catch it or attempt to kill all my boat speed and back-paddle to try to avoid it. The surfboat rower in me decided this was too good to miss and I started to row as hard as I could to ensure a good takeoff. The back of *TTII* lifted in the air seconds before being thrust forward down the massive face of the swell. I felt as though I was flying as *TTII* vibrated with speed — I stopped rowing and slid my seat towards the back of the boat, worried about burying the bow under the water. The ride seemed to go forever and as bubbling foam covered the back of *TTII* I looked at the GPS. We'd hit 13 knots and I decided I'd probably leave the next few waves to let the excitement settle down a bit.

It was 7 p.m. and I only had a hour of light left to decide how I would set the boat up for the evening. With the swell increasing I wondered whether to use the sea anchor but instead I decided that progress was far more important and I let *TTII* run free overnight, hoping for substantial progress.

My torturous night in the cabin rolling free over the swells proved to be a wise decision, gaining 33 km directly towards New Zealand, although my mental state was fairly strained. I was happy with our progress until I received the daily weather forecast. The evil easterlies were on their way again, and this time they were predicted to be stronger and blowing to exactly where I didn't want to go. I was faced with the decision to either throw in the towel and give up on reaching halfway over the next week or attack the storm. I definitely didn't want to be spending time in the cabin again so I decided I'd take the storm head on.

The next day I rowed relentlessly from 6.30 a.m. through until lunch time, battered around by the ocean and making slow progress by tacking across the sea and utilizing the wave direction, while heavily straining the rudder.

With between 25 and 30 knots of wind the conditions were intense and the pressure on my foot rudder control plate increased, until I was broaching down the face of a wave and snapped the plate in two, losing all control of the rudder. As I tried to figure out what was going on, the lack of rudder control was moving me dangerously side on to oncoming waves. I had to move quickly to rig and deploy the sea anchor before I could begin repairs.

Sea anchor duly deployed, *TTII* was jerking from side to side. This was making dismantling the foot plate incredibly challenging, let alone climbing into the bow to retrieve my box of tools and spare parts. The 2 mm stainless-steel foot plate had split in half and I needed to drill four holes through the plate.

On land, with an electric drill and welding machine, this would have been a 10-minute job, but being on the Tasman Sea would see this debacle drag out over five hours as I drilled my way through the plates using a drill bit and pair of needle-nose pliers. By twisting the plate, held firmly in one hand against the pliers, and holding the drill bit in the other hand, each new hole would take an hour and a half to work through as I watched the kilometres I had worked so hard for slowly drift away, until I was back where I'd started from at 6.30 that morning.

I worked on the steering plate for a total of six hours, eventually building a great substitute for the original plate. Dragging some enthusiasm up from somewhere I wanted to test the plate, so I pulled the sea anchor in with waves splashing over the bow and began to row into the southeasterly wind, hoping to at least hold my position. As darkness slowly fell the sea was the biggest and most turbulent I'd seen so far and I had no idea how to deal with the situation.

Slightly nervous about setting up the sea anchor, as I was worried it would rip the front of the boat off, I watched over the stern, wondering how I would get through the night and how much worse the waves and wind were going to get. Not wanting to use the sea anchor out the bow, I thought about filling *TTII* with as much weight as possible and throwing 60 m of rope out

187

the back, hopefully creating enough drag to send her straight down the waves rather than side on.

I found some rope in the bow compartment, took my shorts off and tied them onto the end of the rope to create just a bit more drag, then attached the rope to the bridle over the stern. I threw it overboard, waiting to see the effect. The rope uncoiled as we slid down the first wave and the drag gradually pulled *TTII* straight in line with the face of the wave. Standing on the deck with no pants, I was happy to see it seemed to be working and loaded the hull with more sea water. It was a wild night, with some significantly hair-raising moments, but the extra weight created by the water in the boat and the rope out the back did the job and we got through.

The ferocious sea was unrelenting, with Clouds' text telling me I needed to be careful. The Southern Ocean was blowing north to meet me but even when I was battling through a Tasman tantrum, Mother Nature still calls and I was about to experience my first poo in 45 knots of wind.

Stifled by the sheer inconvenience of the situation, I was dressed in full wet-weather gear and would need to take most of it off on deck in order to drop the kids in the pool. The boat was rocking from side to side and as the odd wave caught *TTII* we would shoot down the front of it.

By this stage I had adopted my favorite bathroom position. Just in front of the bow compartment I set up my bucket with some water, then placed my toilet seat on top ready to begin. My jacket had to come off before I could unclip my overall-style pants, and with rain and waves both pouring in, I knew I was going to get soaked. Which I proceeded to do, but not in the way I had intended.

I sat there, soaking wet and naked with my pants around my ankles, hoping that what I was about to deliver didn't take its time. I braced for a couple of big waves with the icy-cold bucket water sloshing up to meet my backside a few times, but I didn't see a big green wave about to hit us on the side. A wave of water dumped into the cockpit, knocking me completely off my throne and onto the boat deck.

Usually this would be fine, but on this wonderful occasion the bucket decided to empty directly into my pants, which I wouldn't realize until I'd stood and pulled them back up. I admit, I was a bit distracted at the time, with my attention on getting back to the oars and taking control of *TTII*. In hindsight I wish someone else had seen the complete mess I was in, to appreciate how funny it was. After cleaning myself up I was back on the oars chuckling to myself and now well aware of a new risk posed by turbulent conditions. I guess you could say I was well and truly rowing by the seat of my pants that day.

I'd seen a number of seabirds out on the Tasman, the odd flock attacking fish as they swam close to the surface, others just blissfully floating over the larger swells, and I'd never really taken too much notice. As the strong breeze slowly turned into more of a gale, I was greeted by the most amazing and beautiful bird I've ever seen. I like to think of it as a gift from the Tasman for staying outside to battle the storm.

An enormous albatross sliced the front of the steepest waves with its wings. I was astounded at the size of the white bird, as it glided up and down over the wave crests. At times it swooped within a few metres of me and I tried to take photos, but I wasn't fast enough, nor did I think a photo would ever do justice to the sheer marvel of this incredible animal. I rowed along with the albatross keeping me entertained for the afternoon, sharing the waves for the first time in a month and pausing every now and then to watch the aerobatic display.

Due to the weather and the incredibly turbulent sea I had decided not to run the watermaker for a few days, to make sure I didn't run out of power. It was day 31 on the Tasman and the rain had finally receded. Around lunch time I pulled everything wet out of the cabin to dry and switched on the watermaker, happy that the sun would charge the solar battery while the watermaker pumped away.

I spent an hour on deck organizing clothing and bedding, trying to get it all as dry as possible, noticing at the end of it that no water had been produced. I opened the watermaker hatch to see the pump working away. I couldn't see any visible leaks or loose attachments, so put the problem down to bubbles in the system that would hopefully work themselves out if I left it running for a few hours.

But when the watermaker continued pumping without creating any water I was prompted to count up how much water I had left. I had 58 litres and looking back now I can see I was strangely calm about it, perhaps not really taking the situation into account. I was tired and had enough water and food for the night so I went to sleep early, telling Michael there were a few problems with the watermaker but nothing to worry about, and once again attempted to sleep in the bone-jarring ocean.

18 The waves are big in the middle

At 3 a.m. I awoke to the sound of the rudder hitting the side of *TTII*, which sounded like a door slamming. With each side-to-side rock of the boat, another ear-cracking thump came from the stern. With no idea what was going on I groaned, knowing I'd have to take a look and somehow get the situation sorted. Which would start with putting on my soaking wet jacket. Wonderful.

First I checked through the back hatch, which was on the roof of the cabin at the very back of the boat just above the rudder. Climbing through would undoubtedly result in soaking myself and the cabin, as the waves would dump directly on me. Squeezing out the small hole I could see the bubbling white face of the waves but it was almost impossible to judge the size or speed of incoming swells, so I'd have to suss it out and work quickly. The rudder was swinging freely from side to side on the pintles and while thankfully there seemed to be no structural damage, it was obvious one of the steel steering lines had broken in half. I knew that if I left it, as I dozed, each slap of the rudder on the side would become increasingly annoying as I tried to sleep. It was obvious it needed a temporary fix until I could figure out a solution in the morning. Sliding out of the hatch and over my soaking wet bed and blanket, I closed the top hatch and headed out on deck to secure the broken cables.

I was on deck and clipped onto the safety cable running along the deck when I noticed the wire steering line had been pulled out of all the attachment points along the side. There would be no way of securing the rudder unless I got in the water and retrieved the line trailing behind *TTII*. Fortunately, by this stage I *had* learned to slow down and think carefully through all the possible alternatives before jumping overboard at night in massive seas.

Feeling *TTII* move up and down, I put my arm in the water to get an idea of how fast she was actually moving and how much drag I was going to be subjected to if I jumped in to get the line. Sometimes *TTII* was almost still, while other times she tripled in speed when a wave pushed her forwards. I would have to get in the water, grab the line and get out between swells to avoid being dragged behind the boat. Because it was night it would be very difficult to judge the speed of the oncoming waves.

I made the decision to go in based on the danger of the rudder breaking off if it was caught on the wrong angle, and I knew I couldn't afford to risk losing the steering cable as well. I stripped down to Speedos and my lifejacket, with a small personal location device, which was also an EPIRB, taped onto my leg. I attached two safety lines, one around my waist and the other clipped onto the lifejacket, and attached the lines to different strong points on *TTII*. Looking down into the water, it was completely black with the odd glitter of phosphorescence stirred up in the white wash of the waves. I felt cold and nervous about what I was about to do, practically sobbing as I positioned myself to climb into the water after thoroughly rechecking all the attachment points on the boat and me.

Watching the waves, I saw a potential break where I might have time to launch into the water, grab the line and thread it through the attachments before the next wave rolled in. Counting in my head, I knew in this situation it didn't pay to think and it was time to let action and instinct take direct control. A wave rolled under the boat and I climbed into the black sea.

TTII was quickly swept away from me as I swam around the back; I felt a new level of fear as I watched her red and white strobe lights float away and I panicked trying to find the stainless steel wire. I could hear the waves coming as the safety lines were pulled tight and as I was slowly dragged through the water I located the wire line and pulled on the safety lines to locate the attachments on the side of the boat and somehow threaded the line through the four loops.

The entire ordeal was over in a few moments and I climbed back into *TTII* with plenty of time to spare, gratefully tying off the wire cable and locking the rudder in place until morning. Physically, I had only a few small cuts in my soft, wet hands from threading the flayed-out broken wire, but mentally I was a wreck and couldn't believe what I'd just done. I was cold and wet, and moved back into the cabin and into my polar fleece jumper, before trying to sleep. It's fair to say sleep was non-existent that night. Retrieving the lost line had absorbed a few hours and the sun was already starting to try to burn through the grey clouds.

The mental battle to get out of the cabin came back with a vengeance this particular morning. With so much work ahead of me and a potentially broken watermaker, I wasn't sure how to face the day. I spent two hours lying in the cabin rolling from side to side, inspired by nothing at all. I tried to be grateful for what I had but nothing was good and I'm sure I would have spent all day lying there if I hadn't needed to go to the bathroom.

Eventually getting on deck, my attitude improved marginally, helped by a chat to Michael about how halfway was just around the corner and I would be home in no time. I organized breakfast before looking at the broken steering wire and threw around a few ideas in my head about how I could possibly fix the wire, wondering what had broken it in the first place.

The tool kit had a number of different nuts, bolts and clamps and I had the odd bit of wire floating around so I wasn't too worried about fixing it; the challenge was summoning the motivation to deal with the issue. I ended up fixing two lengths of wire together and I found that the pulleys guiding the wire from outside to inside the cockpit were fixed at slightly the wrong angle, wearing the wire and eventually breaking it. I tried to change the angle of the pulley, but it was impossible and I could see that broken steering cables could be an ongoing problem.

Rain continued to bucket down and I decided to leave the watermaker for now as I gave rowing a try. The wind speed had certainly dropped this morning, but because the wind direction seemed to be constantly changing the sea was big, steep and choppy — far worse than 13-m-high consistent swells. By this stage my confidence had definitely increased and I would now attempt rowing in very rough conditions. As my desire to make progress increased limits were starting to be pushed. For every full stroke of the oars *TTII* would rock from side to side and I'd wait, sometimes as long as 10 seconds, to position the oars for the next stroke. On the odd occasion a wave would pick us up I'd suddenly find myself sliding down a steep wave, rowing like mad to try to keep the momentum before falling off the back and having to pull hard to get *TTII* moving in the right direction again. I maintained the correct heading, thinking that any day now I was going to hit the halfway mark and stopping wasn't an option.

Frustration set in a number of times and I would lose my temper, expressing my anger by stupidly rowing as hard as I could for a few moments before eventually regaining my composure and calming down. By the time 3 p.m. ticked around I'd only covered 7 km over the entire day. Catching a wave, I was exhausted and didn't notice another broken wave about to hit me broadside. I caught sight of it at the last moment before it picked up *TTII* by the side, almost rolling her over, while at the same time knocking the oar out of my hand. The oar caught under the hull and snapped in half like a matchstick, leaving me holding the handle.

After unleashing a few choice words I focused on the fact that we didn't flip and I had spare oars. As I started preparing the other oar I tried to work out how to avoid it happening again. I was still putting off dealing with the watermaker and that afternoon I reached into the water compartment and opened the first of my 58 litres of spare water, wondering if I should be thinking about rationing water.

The next day I couldn't help but think about the unfortunate week I was experiencing. With the combination of the broken steering foot plate and cables and the watermaker as well as having to get in the water at 3 a.m., I wasn't having the best run.

Day 33 and the southerly storm slowed down; finally, the weather improved. With smoother seas I knew I had to address the watermaker and I allocated four hours that morning to attack the problem. At this stage I'd gone through five litres of my reserve water, taking my total supply down to 53 litres. The weather was almost perfect for rowing, which added to the frustration of having to repair the watermaker, but also making it possible to take the watermaker apart.

It was an arduous process. Oars hauled in, I laid out a microfibre cloth inside the cabin, along with spare parts for the watermaker and its instruction manual. I had both my tool boxes out and was confident I'd have it running in a matter of hours. Removing the machine involved slowly unbolting eight nuts. I had to meticulously take apart the entire pressurized pumping system and make sure all the seals were working properly, replacing a total of 12 rubber seal O-rings on 10 different moving parts and then make sure all 44 parts went back together perfectly.

I took my time. I was sticking exactly to what the book said, with the entire process eventually taking five hours. It was a job I didn't want to do again and after reconnecting the electric pump I reached into the cabin and flicked the switch. I decided to let the pump run for 40 minutes while I climbed on the oars for the first time that day. I enjoyed the calmer conditions and found the rowing quite relaxing, so I let an hour pass.

The watermaker hadn't produced a drop of water. Fumbling around I tried a number of things suggested by the trouble-shooting guide, but none of them made any difference. I was gutted and dismantled the watermaker yet again. From this point I immediately started to ration water, allocating myself 2.3 litres per day.

When I called Michael at 5 p.m. I told him what was up and recorded a message on my website letting any troubleshooting supporters out there know my watermaker wasn't working, and asking if anyone had any suggestions.

As the message went live on the website Michael began to field a number of media calls about my lack of water and what this meant for the expedition, asking what would be the next step. As neither Michael nor I really knew what to do this was a tricky question.

The weather was improving and I had a text from Clouds telling me I'd have three days of westerly winds, all of which would be reasonable to row and should provide me with enough time to have a solid crack at the halfway mark. Excited at this prospect I decided to leave the watermaker alone while I took advantage of the following conditions.

Over the next three days the conditions, which had been completely calm, slowly built, consistently pushing me in a westerly direction. At midnight on Monday, 22 February 2010, I crossed 163 degrees of longitude and celebrated with a shot of whisky and some rehydrated apple crumble.

By the next day the wind speed had dramatically increased and Clouds sent me a warning that the next night was going to bring the worst conditions I had experienced. The watermaker had to wait — there was no possible way I was going to be able to repair it in the dangerous conditions that were about to hit me.

Clouds was right. The noise of the wind and the waves was like nothing I had heard before and I was absolutely flying towards New Zealand. Just before the sun dropped *TTII* rolled up to the top of an enormous swell and I looked out to see endless breaking waves starting from the horizon and rolling towards me.

Wanting desperately to continue heading towards New Zealand but scared and exhausted, I moved into the cabin, wondering once again what the sea was going to throw at me.

I called Michael and let him know I would delay my report until 9.30 p.m. as he had told me he was going to be busy and I waited, feet braced on the roof as I was struck by wave after wave.

19 Testing times

The noise was like nothing I had ever experienced — it was as though *TTII* was parked next to a steam train blowing its horn. The noise by itself was enough to drive me crazy, as the volume would suddenly increase moments before a wave crashed into the side. I had postponed my check-in call with Michael and I lay on the cabin floor watching the clock and waiting for Clouds to text me about the weather for the evening.

When he did, it was to tell me that things were not looking that good. I could expect a maximum of 50 knots peaking at around midnight then slowly dropping off over the next 24 hours. This was the most powerful wind I had come up against and it would be an interesting test to see if *TTII* could handle the increased wind and waves.

I needed to be moving north at this stage, as the winds and currents of the past 35 days had blown me as far south as Westport on the west coast of the South Island of New Zealand. I was trying to hit the North Island, which at that stage was about another 222 km further north. This prompted my decision not to rig a sea anchor for the night and take the free kilometres on offer from the southwesterly storm.

Rolling free down the massive waves I was hit severely several times by what felt like a bus, but was just another huge wave letting me know I certainly wasn't crossing the Tasman for free. I was unable to cope with what was going on outside and in an attempt to block out the situation I started listening to my iPod, hoping the music would take me somewhere else. I curled up in the very back of the cabin, shaping the wet bean bags around my head to try to block some of the outside noise before turning up the volume to hear Bob Marley's three little birds telling me not to worry, because every little thing was gonna be all right. *TTII* was hit another couple of times, but without the crashing noise of the waves and all the other mysterious and worrisome clunking and rocking noises I was slowly falling asleep as the music soothed my situation.

I had spent 35 days on *TTII* at this stage and was becoming increasingly complacent and overconfident of her ability to take a thrashing in the ferocious sea. I was about to be taught a serious lesson.

At 10.15 p.m. I was woken abruptly as my body was rolled and thrown around inside the cabin. I found myself in among a collection of loose equipment floating in a small amount of water. The cabin was completely black but I could hear water flowing in from somewhere and the water level in the cabin was slowly rising. I got the shock of my life when I took a split second to look out the main cabin hatch and could see nothing but water.

As I quickly gathered my thoughts, my focus was getting out of this situation safely, and how I was going to keep the boat floating and myself alive. In the darkness I fumbled around in the complete mess of junk floating in the water. Finally, I located the main battery switch for the electronics, ripping the wires out to stop any flow of electricity that might short-circuit my equipment.

Next I needed to find out where the water was coming into the cabin. Feeling around in the darkness, I realized it was definitely pouring in from the main cabin hatch. I remembered closing the cabin door that night and could only remember locking off two out of the four latches, which must be what was now allowing water to flow in. I found the latches and began to wrestle with each one, eventually sealing myself inside the submerged and now semi-filled compartment.

I found my head torch and emergency grab bag, and immediately attached an EPIRB to my arm, preparing for the worst. I was sitting in water while it sloshed around on the roof of my cabin and everything in my cabin was now floating around me.

TTII had been flipped end over end by a massive wave, burying her nose at the bottom while the rest of the wave picked her up and flicked us completely over. I'd hit my face fairly hard on the cabin roof and was currently upside down in the middle of the Tasman at 10.30 p.m. in a 7-metre-long boat that wasn't flipping back up.

TTII was very still now, with only a small portion of her hull sticking out of the water. I took a few deep breaths to calm myself and started assessing the situation. There was no more water coming into the cabin but there was already a significant amount, adding a substantial weight to the roof of the cabin, which was now the lowest point under the water. *TTII* was designed and built to roll and almost immediately pop back up again. On this occasion the water in the cabin was acting as ballast and would hold *TTII* upside down unless I could manoeuvre my weight around or create enough rocking from inside the cabin to shift the water, when *TTII* should hopefully pop back up again.

I placed my feet on one side of the cabin wall and shuffled up with my back against the opposite cabin wall until I was almost flat against the cabin floor, which was now the roof. After slipping down a number of times I managed to find a good position and I tried rocking *TTII* from side to side. As I rocked back and forwards from inside the cabin I watched the water level on the cabin door like a hawk — if I got the timing right a proportion of the cabin hatch would rise out of the water before dropping back beneath the surface.

After rocking the boat for 10 minutes without success I began to develop a sick feeling in my stomach that perhaps the expedition was over and I needed help. Adding to this horrific feeling was the thought that I had possibly lost all my oars and life raft off the deck as well as my sunglasses. What I didn't know at that time was that as *TTII* was launched end over end, my tracking beacon fixed to the top of *TTII* was submerged. It had immediately sent a distress signal visible only on my website.

In all my website and safety planning, I'd forgotten that this distress signal would be visible to anyone following the website, including the media. As I had missed my prearranged 9.30 p.m. call with Michael he was already concerned and was stuck next to his phone when he received a call from the New Zealand Rescue Coordination Centre asking him if he'd heard from me as a distress signal had been set off.

By now I'd been capsized for about 15 minutes and decided to move all the weight to one side of the cabin and try rocking backwards and forwards again; hopefully, this time I could create a stronger rocking motion. Positioned on the roof again I moved my weight back and forward relentlessly, almost reaching the point where she would pop up. I realized I was going to need the assistance of a wave to push me over as well as rocking from the cabin and this meant I would need to keep rocking the boat for as long as it took to catch a lucky wave. Back and forward we went, with water and equipment moving around the dark cabin and my soggy feet slipping down the wall. It was an agonizing wait until *TTII* was quickly lifted past a particular point and then incredibly slowly she eased back over and I was once again on the cabin floor, covered in water and equipment.

I didn't celebrate for a second as I knew I would only have a brief time to empty the cabin of all the water before I was hit again. I began to bail furiously with one hand as the other hand was locked tight on the main cabin door, ready to pull it shut if another wave hit us. Taking another 10 minutes to bail the boat out, I made sure I was completely sealed in before I grabbed my waterproof hand-held GPS to establish my exact coordinates before calling Michael.

By this stage I was starting to shake from the shock of the situation and dialling the numbers on the satellite phone was very difficult. The phone rang once before Michael answered. I relayed my position and provided a quick update before telling him to let the Rescue Coordination Centre know my position, and ask if they would please call me.

At this stage I was unsure what equipment I did or didn't have and before I spoke to the Rescue Coordination Centre I wanted to be able to provide an accurate assessment. Rushing and not thinking straight I opened the cabin door and stepped outside on deck, noticing the life raft was dragging behind. Still attached inside its bag, it was being pulled along by one very thin piece of rope, and I was horrified to see the oars were dangling over the side.

I panicked, and without a lifejacket or tether line, started recklessly hauling in the various pieces of equipment, leaning almost into the water in an attempt to get the life raft on board and my oars back on deck. The life raft weighed 30 kg on its own, let alone what it was pulling as it was being dragged behind the boat. To get it in I used the same technique used to pull a patient into a surf-lifesaving rescue boat — pushing the life raft underwater and using its own buoyancy to help lift it up over the gunwales. I slipped doing it and almost fell out of the boat on the opposite side. The oars were light and easy by comparison, but another one had snapped and securing them in the boat was now more important than ever, as I was down to my last set.

Moving around the deck I noticed the middle storage compartment had burst open and I could see I'd lost some of my water. As I started to go and take a closer look I also realized I was out on deck unsecured and without any protection and that I was being incredibly reckless, so I jumped back into the cabin, sealing the door behind me.

As I waited for the call from the Rescue Coordination Centre I tried to dry my hands but everything was wet so I had to use the satellite phone inside its plastic bag. I answered the phone and was asked to provide my position and give a brief description of my situation and if I required assistance.

The temptation to give up had never been more intense. I was tired and wet and there were still about two more days left in the storm. I couldn't help thinking about myself in a warm bed, just waiting for me a tempting 24 hours away. I managed to dull my immediate reaction and decided to wait until 10 o'clock the next morning to make the decision about whether or not I would continue.

By this stage Michael had already received a number of calls from the media, blocking his phone as I attempted to call him again. I knew Michael would let the others know I was OK but at this point I decided to call Lisa, who I knew would also be worried.

What I thought would be quite an emotional phone call was very robotic and must have sounded rehearsed, as I reassured her everything was fine and under control. I was very lucky that we had a wonderful flatmate, Catherine Allan, who I relied on to look after Lisa. I found out later that the media started to call Lisa from 3 a.m. that particular morning and she answered one call before taking the phone off the wall.

At this stage everyone important knew where I was and what my situation was, so I turned off the phone and the lights and wondered how the rest of the night would play out. The waves still thundered onto and over me and I considered what I would say to the RCC the next morning, when they asked me if I could continue.

When the time came to make the call I hadn't slept at all and everything around me was dripping wet. Thankfully, the sun eventually appeared and I went outside to see what *TTII* had lost in the flip.

At first glance everything looked OK but we were down one oar, a hat and a pair of sunglasses. Both the radio aerials had snapped off and I'd lost my radar reflector, all of which were quite minor in comparison to what I found next, when I checked the centre storage compartment that had busted open during the flip.

Of course it had to be the one with my spare water and 30 of those vital litres had floated free while I was upside down. This could spell the end of the crossing. With only 15 litres of water left and still 890 km away from land I would probably not survive rowing on that small amount of water.

All the drama and shock of the past 12 hours hit me and I was a blubbering mess once again, with no idea how I would keep going. I couldn't bear the thought of going back into my cabin and I tried to gather my thoughts, but at this stage it was better to let the tension out until I was ready to get on with it.

I called a number of people that morning and vented my emotion to them in an attempt to change my own mindset. Everyone I spoke to was incredibly supportive as I cried down the phone to various mates and family. The worst part about sitting there in my wet boat was that I knew deep down there were a number of things I could do, and I would be continuing no matter what, but home was still a very distant place from my little boat.

My entire perception changed after a text message from Steven Gates, the best Australian in the world, who had driven my boat up to Coffs Harbour.

I heard you took a flip, YOU LUCKY BASTARD! We were never fortunate enough, onwards and upwards.

All the other messages had been messages of sympathy, and his was exactly what I needed to change the paradigm my mind had created. Within moments I embraced the fact that I'd flipped with *TTII* and we'd both survived. We were in the middle of the Tasman and life had officially become extreme! My mind switched from doomsday depression to positive solution-finding focus and I thought of all the ways I could collect water, including the possibility of rendezvousing with a yacht or another boat over the next 10 or so days. Once again everything seemed possible. I phoned Michael and told him I'd have another go at fixing the watermaker.

I called Lisa too, who only moments earlier had put up with me crying down the phone.

When the RCC got through, they told me I could be picked up that afternoon by a passing container ship and be home the next day. After pausing for a second I said I would be continuing under the power of my own oars and and thanked them for their offer of assistance. Saying no to the rescue made me feel low again as I visualized climbing off the container ship and into a warm bed but I balanced this by focusing on what it would feel like standing on a beach as the first person to row from Australia to New Zealand, which hopefully now wasn't that far away.

With 15 litres of water left, rationing would have to be strict and I decided I would only drink 1 litre a day until I came up with a solution. This would most definitely restrict my physical ability but I would only drink more if I was dizzy or delirious.

I waited till lunch time to call Dad and discuss the capsize with him, which tested my emotions. Dad was great at talking through exactly what had happened with me, and we discussed a few strategies to try to avoid it happening again.

With the increased media attention Michael had now fielded over 200 phone calls and emails asking for press releases and information. As a result I now had an entire community of different people around the world working on what the problem with my watermaker might be, and they were all contacting Michael with lots of ideas.

Rather than attempt to fix the watermaker straight away I felt my time over the next two days would be better spent taking advantage of the prevailing winds and rowing as hard as I could towards New Zealand; hopefully, some good progress would give me a psychological boost. I could certainly do with one.

I rowed incredibly hard, as if I was trying to win something back from the Tasman for what it had done to me the night before, and shooting down the face of one wave claimed what would end up being my highest recorded speed — 15.3 knots down the towering swell. By 7 p.m. I had travelled 44 km over five hours, which was fantastic progress, but now I would have to start thinking about heading back into the cabin. By this stage I was incredibly tired and getting increasingly cold.

It was as if I was climbing into the cabin for the first time. Once again I had to rebuild resistance to my fears of capsizing and being trapped in the small space, only this time I knew *exactly* what there was to worry about. Although I was incredibly scared I didn't want to slow the boat down with the sea anchor, as we were moving very quickly in the correct direction. I had decided earlier on with Dad that one of the possible reasons I flipped was that the back of the boat was too light and being lifted out of the water. He suggested I should think about putting the small parachute anchor out the back of the boat to hold her down on the water's surface.

Having never done this before I was slightly apprehensive, but the theory was sound and I needed to do something to ease my mind and get some sort of rest overnight.

Climbing into the bow cabin I found the small parachute anchor, which was a funnel-shaped drogue, 40 cm wide, and worked out how I would attach it and rig it off the back of the cabin. Attaching 30 m of rope, I slowly released the chute and was surprised at how quickly it shot out the back of the boat. The big sea anchor had never shot away so quickly and tension quickly snapped the line tight as *TTII* reduced speed.

Rather than waves crashing over the front, now they crashed over the back. I wasn't sure if this was really a good or bad thing, and wouldn't know until I gathered the strength to climb back into the cabin for my first night after the capsize.

Inside the cabin it sounded like the parachute was about to rip the entire cabin off as we were pulled through some waves backwards. At other times the line would wrap around the rudder and I had to lean out the back hatch and use the broken oar to slide the tangled rope down the rudder. The parachute drogue out the back of the boat was certainly effective, and although it did reduce boat speed dramatically, it was essential for stopping *TTII* flipping again. This provided some new and different boat movements to get used to, and something else to be fearful about, but it certainly did the job and we still managed to make 31 km over the night.

In the days following the capsize I was fortunate enough to experience some fantastic rowing conditions, so rather than stop and take the watermaker apart I continued to row, making as much distance towards New Zealand as possible. The reasoning behind this was that it would put me into a far better position if I did happen to need assistance.

By now I was rowing in line with the very top of the South Island of New Zealand. While the day was dark, thankfully there was no rain so I was able to dry the odd item of clothing, as everything I had was still soaking wet. As well as losing a significant amount of weight I had a number of sores and blisters making everyday movement painful, so I was lying on my stomach with my backside exposed trying to air out the various infections plaguing my comfort. The seas had dropped significantly and Clouds told me that the next day would be almost completely flat with no wind. This was great as I needed to dry out the entire cabin and everything in it, so I decided that tomorrow would almost certainly be my first laundry day.

But my scary week wasn't over. Late that evening I was rowing at a fairly standard pace of about 1.3 knots when a huge fin popped up out of the water, trailed behind the boat and then disappeared. Slightly scared, I stopped rowing, not wanting the splashes to attract any unwanted attention. I held my breath and slowly glided with the momentum of the boat, waiting a long silent moment before carefully peering over the side. Nothing. I decided to start rowing again. After just three strokes the huge fin appeared again, this time slicing the water between where my rowing blade hit the water and the side of *TTII*.

I jumped in my seat, slightly frightened, and left the oar hanging a few moments before regaining my composure. I slowly began rowing again, wondering what else the Tasman had in store for me. Over the past seven days I'd broken my watermaker, capsized the boat, snapped a steering cable and lost more than half my drinking water.

Fortunately, nothing else happened. Later on I was told I was in for a smooth night and I might finally manage to get some much-needed sleep. The next lot of bad weather wasn't due for another five days, and with only 8 litres of water left a decision needed to be made. There was no rain forecast and the water-maker still wasn't working.

Putting all my eggs in one basket, I convinced myself I'd be able to fix the problem. With that in mind I took advantage of the calm weather and went to sleep.

20 Water, water everywhere but not a drop …

The next day I woke up from the best sleep I'd experienced on the Tasman so far, a solid five hours completely uninterrupted, which made me feel absolutely amazing. Quickly getting out of bed and into a hot bowl of porridge I tried to hold onto that enthusiasm for as long as I could. The Tasman was almost completely dead flat and the sky looked as though it fell directly into the sea on the horizon, with the blue of the sky and sea a perfect match. As soon as the sun rose over the line of the horizon it started to get very hot; I was dreading having to row today because I knew I had to ration my water and that would be increasingly hard to manage if it was hot.

When planning the expedition, in my ignorance I thought completely calm days would be fantastic for progress, but they proved to be terrible. I would have to work very hard all day with my top speed only just bettering 2 knots if there was a small swell running. I covered myself in sunblock and put on a long-sleeved shirt and leggings. My favourite hat and sunglasses had gone missing after the capsize and I squinted all day, until the sun eventually set.

As the hours passed the silence would be the most amazing thing, with the only noise coming from the odd fish jumping

211

or a whale taking a breath a few kilometres away. I would sometimes stop and close my eyes and try to listen for a sound — any sort of sound! With lunch time approaching I'd only made 15 km over five hours, which was fairly slow, and I decided rather than waste the energy and drinking water, I would start to work on maintenance.

Still avoiding the watermaker issue, I decided to scrub the bottom of the hull again, seeing as it was a beautifully smooth day. I had opened up all the hatches and strung a line across the boat to hang up my clothes after washing them all in salt water and letting them drip dry in the sun. *TTII* looked like someone's dirty house, with everything spread everywhere, including wet manuals, clothing, rope, first-aid equipment — even my soggy toilet paper had its place on the deck, soaking up the sun.

I had found my goggles and paint scraper and this time I decided to take some wet and dry sandpaper underneath as well to make sure I was squeezing every last inch of speed out of *TTII*. I checked around for bitey things for a solid 20 minutes before slowly lowering myself into the water. Once I was in I spent the next 10 minutes feeling very wary, remembering that massive fin I'd seen a few days earlier. I was hoping like hell that whatever it belonged to hadn't been following me.

Scrubbing vigorously, I was incredibly thorough in getting every single bit of growth off, sanding and scraping the surface completely smooth, while constantly looking over my shoulder for anything that could eat me. I soon noticed that as I was significantly further south by this time, the water temperature had dropped. Any longer than 15 minutes in the water and I'd start shivering and would need to hop out and row for a bit to warm up.

Altogether I spent about two hours cleaning the bottom

212

with the very cold water adding a few extra challenges, before I couldn't avoid it any longer and knew it was time to deal with the watermaker. The temperature was noticeably colder as the sun disappeared lower in the sky and I moved everything inside and climbed into my wet-weather clothing before rowing for an hour to warm up. Happy that I was getting a bit more speed from *TTII* after the big clean, I extended my hour and rowed for close to three, before eventually hauling in the oars, opening my tool boxes and finally tackling the watermaker.

I called Michael and asked him to read out what people who'd emailed thought the problem might be, and their ideas about how I could possibly repair it. As Michael was speaking I took notes, then later started unbolting the pump and filter from inside the small compartment. I'd tested the power and eliminated the possibility of the battery being too weak, so the problem had to be inside the unit. I had to take the machine apart again and check all the different seals. Because I knew what I was doing this time it only took two and a half hours to take it apart and put it back together again. As I was reconnecting the power I decided to let the unit run for an hour and see if it would work.

I rowed for a short while, watching the salt-water pump through the pipes, all the while hoping it would work its way through the system and produce some drinking water. An hour went past and the watermaker was producing nothing. Not a drop. Now incredibly frustrated, I worked through the troubleshooting manual again and called Michael to see if he had any more ideas, which again resulted in me dismantling the unit to make sure I had replaced all the parts *exactly* perfectly. The sun had disappeared and I had been sitting still for six hours playing with this machine and was incredibly cold.

I gave up on the machine, packing it away before boiling some water and taking it into the cabin with me to warm up. Once I'd warmed up a bit I called Michael and told him the watermaker still wasn't working, and that I'd try again tomorrow.

He told me he'd been contacted by John Funnell, who owned a helicopter and a few planes. He and his son Mark, who was also a pilot, were thinking about flying out to me.

With the weather looking very unpredictable over the next 10 days I could quite easily be blown back towards Australia, and more importantly I wouldn't be able to receive any assistance. John Funnell is incredibly experienced at this sort of flying, and had already been involved with long-distance rescues, so I knew this wasn't an offer to take lightly. By now I only had 4 litres of drinking water and with 500 km still to row things were getting a bit desperate. I asked John and his son if they would be able to organize an air drop of water and when he said he'd give it a go the relief was immense.

John Funnell's account

For my part, I was contacted by RCCNZ and asked if I had a helicopter that could get to you the day after you capsized. At first glance it was borderline of being within our range of action, and it all depended on the wind conditions, as that can reduce our flying range.

It was at this stage they said you were getting low on water. When I asked why we weren't thinking about resupplying you with water, they said they were essentially a search and rescue organization, and unless you called for assistance, they couldn't do anything; at that stage they suspected that if you did decide to call for help, it would be to take you off *TTII*.

I then had a closer look at your website and thought, 'This boy has got form and he's over three-quarters of the way home, he's a Kiwi and I want to be part of the team that makes sure he gets home.' I emailed Michael and told him we could deliver water. He told me you were still trying to fix the watermaker and the following Monday evening you were expecting a call from the manufacturer, to try to analyse what needed repairing.

As the week progressed it was becoming obvious that you would need our services, so we organized with the Taupo Coast Guard to do some trials to hone up our aiming skills. We also wanted to try out robust containers with various amounts of packing, to see if we could avoid the use of a parachute, as this is more risky when deployed from an aircraft, let alone the little aircraft we planned to use.

These trials were flown on the Saturday and were a total disaster. None of the 30-litre plastic containers survived the drop test. Sir Barnes Wallis, inventor of the bouncing bombs the Dambusters used in WW2, would have been impressed as these containers bounced across the water on Lake Taupo. Had there been a dam to blow up at the end of their run we may have been very successful.

I thought, 'Well, we're going to have to use parachutes. The issues here is if it opens as it goes out the door it can go over the top of the tail of the aircraft, and the float, with 180 metres of floating line and a 30-litre container, will go under the tailplane. Had this occurred you would have ended up rescuing us.

Sunday afternoon I went and saw Hamish, a pilot and

skydiver who runs Taupo Tandem Skydiving. He said, 'No problem, I can design a static line system that will open the parachute once it is below the aircraft.'

Monday morning saw him dismantling some old parachute harnesses to make three static line systems. This was completed by Monday evening, and Tuesday morning Mark and I did a test on Taupo airport. Not a drop of water was lost, even landing on hard ground. I rang Michael and said we are all set to go.

He replied, 'Good, because Shaun can't fix the water-maker.'

I spoke to you that day on the satellite phone and arranged the Wednesday resupply. That evening Chrissy (my wife) and I were making up the 180 metre lines and winding them into plastic containers so they would feed out without tangling, cooking a surprise roast chicken, purchasing more water as we had lost all the trial water bottles, some coffee, a toothbrush plus some cake and anything else Chrissy could squeeze in, then packing the containers with polystyrene balls to absorb the impact.

Wednesday morning, we left Taupo for New Plymouth to refuel, check your position and headed out to find you. Three hours later we saw the red *TTII* after a text update from Michael 20 minutes earlier, via the satellite phone.

It was about 1 p.m. in the afternoon before I heard the buzz of John and his son Mark's plane coming towards me, tilting their wings as they performed a low pass over the bow. I grabbed the radio and immediately tried calling them, ignoring all the usual radio protocol and starting my conversation with, 'Awesome — it's people, it's actually people!' Clearly, I was slightly more ecstatic to see them than they were to see me. Mark Funnell replied, saying they would begin preparing for the drop. The small plane flew off into the distance preparing for its first approach.

I'd discussed with John about exactly how the drop would take place and the plan was that they would fly 200 m in front of *TTII* in the direction I was rowing, dropping the line in the path of where I was heading. My job would be to row up to the floating line in the sea and pull the barrels and excess line into *TTII*.

John radioed me again saying that the plane had turned and they were heading towards me for the first time. I could see the plane in the distance and I started slowly rowing forward, keeping an eye on the plane as it flew towards me. I could see the small red buoy with the yellow floating nylon line flowing out from the back of the plane, still attached as the plane rocked side to side in the wind. As the plane approached the engines began to roar as if Mark was accelerating. I looked behind to see John push the first barrel out the plane door and the small parachute slowed the barrel's descent. At first I panicked, rowing as hard as I could towards the barrel, slipping off my seat a number of times.

I rowed directly between the floating red buoy and the white water-filled barrel, threw my oars inboard and started hauling in the 200 m of line. The parachute attached to the barrels filled with water and made pulling the line in twice as heavy, but after five minutes I had the barrel next to the boat and lifted it in, waving at John and Mark up in the plane as they circled to see if I'd been able to pick up the barrel.

Once it was in the boat I jumped on the radio to tell John to start getting ready for the next drop and he very sensibly asked me to check the contents first and tell him if the water had survived. I whipped the top off the barrel and saw a packet of candy as well as a newspaper and was rapt to see all of the water had survived. I told him, thanking them for the extra treats as they started preparing for the next drop, going on to repeat the successful fly past and dropping the barrel perfectly.

John and Mark performed a total of three drops, all of which were perfect and the best part about what they had dropped was yet to come. The plane circled a number of times as the crew took photos of *TTII* and a small amount of video footage. It was great to have someone on the end of the radio and for the first time in 42 days I felt as if I had some company.

The guys decided to leave and just as quickly as they had arrived the plane and my new best friends had gone home to their beds for the night and it was back to being alone on the Tasman.

I will never forget receiving that water drop and the massive effort John's family went to, ensuring my expedition could continue. The plane was gone and now it was time to unload the barrels as there was quite the mess on deck by now, with 600 m of nylon rope tangled all over the place. Like opening a present politely, I attempted to untangle the rope before getting frustrated and cutting the barrels free. I unscrewed the lid of the first one and found that John had filled the barrels with polystyrene balls to absorb the impact of the air drop. The first barrel had two blocks of chocolate, a newspaper and a toothbrush. The second barrel had a pack of 'pick and mix' candy and some coffee. In the third barrel I opened, tucked very nicely under another piece of newspaper was an entire roast chicken! I took a moment to comprehend what I was actually looking at before ripping open the packet and taking

218

a huge bite. I can guarantee that will forever be the best piece of chicken I will *ever* taste. In total John and his family had delivered 38 litres of life-saving water, enabling me to continue towards New Zealand — and brush my teeth for the first time in 39 days.

I now had 40 litres of water and I decided I wouldn't bother even looking at the watermaker again until I was down to five litres; over the next week I would focus entirely on making progress towards New Zealand. I spoke to Clouds on the phone that evening and he let me know I needed to get as close to home as possible because a powerful tropical low looked as though it was heading straight towards me and would most certainly push me back towards Australia.

Clouds was successful at putting the fear of god into me and over the next 36 hours I managed to row 150 km towards New Zealand, only having to stop once to repair another broken steering cable. I was now officially down to my last 500 km and exactly in line with Taranaki, which had always been my preferred landing spot. Clouds told me I had five days of strong southwesterlies ahead and I would need to make a strong push east. For the first time it felt like a push for home and for the next seven days my only thought was to try to hit the shores of my beautiful New Zealand.

21 I'm going to bloody miss

Day 44 and with 500 km to go, I had now covered close to 2600 km of the Tasman Sea. Clouds had just informed me I was going to experience around four or five days of easterly winds, which would halt my progress or at worst push me back towards Australia. At this stage I feared nothing more than the prospect of being stuck in my cabin while I was pushed backwards. With New Zealand just within my reach I made a decision to fight as hard as I could to make progress through the easterlies.

Speaking to Michael on the phone that evening, we discussed where we thought I was going to land and at this stage I was still in line with Taranaki — sitting between 39 and 40 degrees of latitude. Michael told me I was on the front page of the paper in New Plymouth and that the entire place was expecting me to land there sometime soon. Not wanting to disappoint an entire city, and anticipating the approaching easterly winds, I decided to row until midnight to make sure I made as much progress towards Taranaki as I could, using the following winds.

As the night progressed the westerly started to turn into more of a southerly and made progress increasingly difficult. I was being blown further and further north and I battled for a short while before deciding to head into the cabin.

The next two days were very similar, as the predominant

wind was coming from the south. I would spend both days battling with the wind to try to hold my ground, managing to make a small amount of progress towards the New Zealand coast.

On the evening of day 46 I was joined by a pod of pilot whales that were about the same length as *TTII* and for about 20 minutes I didn't care where I was rowing, as long as I was sharing the waves with my mates. The small whales would pop their heads out of the water next to *TTII* to make sure they were still keeping up and it would almost look as if they were giving me a wink as their heads broke the surface. My new friends didn't stay around for very long, disappearing again into the deep, and I turned *TTII* around to get back on course.

The next day the easterly winds arrived. I managed to battle for a few hours before almost snapping an oar and deciding to head inside the cabin, not wanting to risk breaking my last set. While I was being thrown around inside the cabin nature called and I would again have to head out on deck at an incredibly inconvenient time, only to discover I'd run out of toilet paper. Not knowing what else to do I improvised, cutting the sleeves off my shirt and making do with a new and improved short-sleeved T-shirt and a new supply of 'toilet paper'.

Back in the cabin I was watching the latitude constantly decrease, which meant I was heading further and further north and by morning I was directly off the coast of Auckland, which meant I'd drifted a total of 300 km north over four days, without making any progress towards land.

When planning the expedition, the prospect of missing New Zealand completely had never occurred to me and now that was I faced with this dilemma I had to attack and start pushing even harder towards home. I called Clouds to find out what the next five were bringing my way. The forecast wasn't good, with another two days of southeasterlies, which meant I wouldn't be making much headway.

I was incredibly stressed by the prospect of not completing the journey after coming so far and my thoughts were constantly about making *TTII* as efficient as possible going towards home and as heavy and slow as possible when I was being blown away.

Having been blown so far north in just four days I knew I needed to slow *TTII* down somehow, so I decided to partially sink her by filling all the centre storage compartments with water, adding around another 150 kg of weight to try to reduce the effect of the wind, which was still insisting on blowing me north.

The combination of this extra weight and putting out the sea anchor slowed the northerly drift from about 1.9 knots down to 0.8 knots, effectively halving my total speed. While that was good, attempting to row southeast with the increased weight was incredibly challenging and made almost no difference at all.

Day 49 was a Tuesday, and the only direction I had moved over the past three days was north, but thankfully due to the curve of the North Island I had actually made 185 km towards land.

Clouds told me this would be the last time I would experience easterly winds for the next six days and I should prepare to row the hardest I've ever rowed if I wanted to avoid crossing the top of the North Island.

As I was being swept up the west coast of New Zealand my

land crew was having an absolute nightmare, trying to predict exactly where and when I was going to land. We'd already announced four different landing locations to the media, starting with Taranaki, then moving to Raglan, then it was the Manukau Bar and now it looked like either the Kaipara or Hokianga Harbours.

With each new location Michael, Lisa and Olly had to call various local coast guards and local fishermen to brief me on potential landing sites and rescue strategies in case I was blown onto rocks in their area. As well as trying to figure out if I could actually land at these various points, the land crew was liaising with sponsors and over 40 different media agencies, keeping everyone in the loop with exactly what was happening to me and where I might end up, which was changing every day.

With Clouds predicting a wind change the next day I was preparing to start my assault towards the New Zealand coast, getting *TTII* and myself ready. I jumped overboard and cleaned the hull, scrubbing every square centimetre to make sure the next few days would be all about speed.

Next morning the easterly wind changed into a slightly less vigorous southwesterly and I began to make some progress. Clouds suggested I row through the night on this particular occasion, because for every kilometre I made towards New Zealand I was also heading the same distance north. When I stopped rowing I only headed north. I battled through until about 11.45 p.m., when I started getting very cold and tired and decided I would again partially sink the boat and put out the sea anchor while I slept.

Back on dry land it was now Thursday and the first day of the New Zealand Surf Life Saving Championships, a weekend I would usually never miss. I drew a certain amount of motivation from the fact that all of my best mates, including Michael, would be racing down at the Nationals and I decided to have my own race over the next few days and push hard towards New Zealand.

As I was drifting up the coast it looked as though I was heading for the Hokianga Harbour, the point Dad had departed from some 34 years earlier on his Tasman crossing. I now desperately wanted to finish by rowing in at the place where Dad had started from. Although an incredibly dangerous landing point, the synergy of sharing it with him would have been magic. Clouds' text message to me that evening told me I was 200 km off the coast of New Zealand and there was only 125 km of New Zealand's northern tip left. I needed to row my guts out because the weather was going to get increasingly worse as I came closer to the coast.

My land crew at this stage was struggling to figure out exactly where they needed to be and with the increasing number of possible landing sights, Lisa had spent the week booking different hotels and motels up the coast, constantly changing the bookings as I headed further north.

Michael and Olly were bombarded with phone calls from the media and over in Australia Patrick was also fielding a barrage of Australian and international media calls, all wanting to know when and where I was going to land. Sitting in my cabin having a small break I decided to rehearse a landing while I still had energy, and created a list of everything I needed to remember if I crash-landed in the middle of the night. This included how exactly I would keep myself warm on the beach and tell my land crew where I was.

It was time for the final push home. New Zealand was 120 km

away and although I couldn't see the land, the colour of the water had changed to a lighter blue. I was beginning to see the odd strange object floating in the water, the strangest of which was a pear bobbing past. I called Michael that evening to tell him that the next few days I wouldn't be communicating much during the day as I wanted to concentrate on rowing as hard as I could. He assured me everything was under control on land and I was going be home soon.

Sadly, Michael wasn't going to be able to make it to the landing point due to the surf-lifesaving champs. He was an integral part of his team and I completely understood his reasons, although I would be gutted not to see him on the beach.

Day 52 and Friday morning — I decided to hit the go button and made a commitment to not stop rowing until I hit land. It was as though I could hear one of my old rugby coaches telling me I was to leave nothing on the park and this was the deciding moment in the game. I had the same distance left *of* New Zealand as I had to row *towards* New Zealand and every moment I stopped I was losing ground.

I slowly chipped away until 1 p.m. and realized I still wasn't going fast enough and needed to get rid of some more weight. I rummaged through *TTII*, throwing almost all my spare food overboard and decided to remove the last of my lead ballast weights. I knew this was a massive risk, as these were responsible for ensuring *TTII* would pop back up again if she rolled, but the result was that *TTII* was now 42 kg lighter, sitting a bit higher in the water and moving faster.

That night I took a small break to call Lisa, who had been working hard coordinating and communicating with a number of people, including my family, making sure they all knew where I was going to end up and who would be involved with the arrival party. Lisa was also in charge of making the call for everyone to start heading north. With my progress making landing incredibly unpredictable, she finally made the call and decided everyone should start heading north early Saturday morning.

I had always made everyone aware that the landing would be the most dangerous part of the expedition and the pressure was on Lisa and Olly to not only liaise with media but also family and rescue coordinators. From about a week earlier we had been discussing all the different people I needed to be involved with a potential beach crash-landing and with the strong possibility of surf life guards heading out in inflatable boats in the middle of the night, it was essential I had a team of highly skilled people ready and willing to respond.

I continued to row, making slow but steady progress towards the very top of the North Island, at this stage rowing in what felt like a slightly possessed trance — not wanting or willing to stop for anything. The seas began to increase in size and I was constantly hunting the horizon for sight of land and day and night blended into one. As my last gas cooking canister ran dry my diet changed to cold porridge and NoDoz caffeine tablets, which saved time and gave me the small energy boost I needed.

Day 53 and as the sun rose I had rowed all night. The surf had constantly increased, almost rolling the now underweight *TTII* a number of times. I no longer cared about the prospect of rolling, feeling that everything should be sacrificed for progress, otherwise it would all have been for nothing.

Scanning the horizon for sight of land I was slightly gutted to find I was 50 km away from the coast and 45 km away from the top of the North Island and I still couldn't see anything but sea. My entire body was hurting — I had just rowed for 24 hours with only a few breaks and the NoDoz and cold porridge wasn't working as well as some much needed anti-inflammatory pills probably would have. I was greeted by a seagull soaring above me and was briefly reminded of *Jonathan Livingston Seagull*, a beautiful book about freedom and adventure Dad had given me to take across the Tasman.

I took a few moments to call Lisa, who by now was driving from Auckland with a convoy of trucks and inflatable rescue boats. I gave her an update of my position and we talked about possible landing sights. Lisa's father, Winton Jones, had taken the role of trying to pinpoint the spot where I was going to land, and when, based on my ongoing progress.

By lunch time it was obvious I was either going to drift over the top of New Zealand or hit somewhere along the coast, on Ninety Mile Beach. I decided it would be a good idea to call the Rescue Coordination Centre and ask what my options were if I was to drift over the top. The not very reassuring answer was that there were no rescue craft capable of getting to me and my best option would be to work as hard as I could to reach land before that happened.

I would again have to step my work rate up another few levels and continue my relentless push to hit the beach. The absolute rawness of the situation was starting to hit home as the waves became steeper with the now shallower water, and started crashing onto *TTII*. I took a moment to think about Andrew McAuley, an Australian kayaker who disappeared only a few kilometres off the South Island west coast after attempting a similar solo Tasman crossing only a few years earlier. I quickly checked all my safety lines and made sure I had an EPIRB attached to me in case I did go overboard.

Around 2.30 in the afternoon I heard a strange noise in the distance and I looked over my shoulder to see a helicopter approaching. The helicopter hovered over the top of *TTII* and I managed to contact them on the radio and asked if they had brought me any dinner. The helicopter was quickly joined by a small plane flown by John Funnell, who had arranged the water drop a few weeks earlier. Civilization was on my doorstep for the first time in 53 days and I know I should have been really over the moon and absolutely ecstatic about landing. And although I *was* excited about seeing people, the Tasman had become the norm for me and the thought of landing and getting back to land and the 'normal' world was ever so slightly intimidating.

After seeing the two aircraft I began to think that this really was going to be my last night on the Tasman Sea and I called Lisa to report my position and get an update on the landing party. The landing was going to be a coordinated effort by a collection of people and Lisa and Olly would have to organize it all. With Michael away at the Nationals, Olly took charge of the media, communicating with the television stations and talking with a few of the locals, arranging Internet for tracking purposes.

Lisa was working with her dad and brother Riley, plotting possible landing sites as well with all my surf-lifesaving friends, who had arrived with essential equipment such as rescue boats and night-lights, preparing for the worst-case scenario of a midnight landing. At about 8 p.m. Lisa called a meeting, letting everyone know I had increased my speed dramatically and if I maintained my speed and course, I could possibly be landing between 2 a.m. and 3 a.m., in which case everyone would need to be up the far end of the beach, which was about a 40 km drive.

TTII had certainly increased her speed and the southerly wind had turned into a 30 knot westerly. I was absolutely flying towards the beach, at some points reaching 5 or 6 knots. I wasn't sure whether I should continue forward and risk a middle-of-the-night crash-landing or if slowing down and waiting for daylight would be the best idea.

I spoke to Michael, who told me he'd won gold in a number of surf events, which was fantastic to hear, and gave me some words of encouragement about this being my last night and how he didn't want the 8 a.m. and 8 p.m. phone calls to stop.

I called Lisa again around 9 p.m. and we discussed what a night landing would involve. I had no problem with crashing onto the beach in the dark, but I knew I'd never forgive myself if one of my mates was injured in the process. I also thought I owed it to *TTII* to get her into shore safely.

I decided to deploy the sea anchor and slow down for the night, resting for the first time in 48 hours. By now I was starting to feel incredibly excited about being home and I certainly wasn't going to sleep. Lisa passed on my decision to everyone involved with the landing and asked them to meet at the local school at 5 o'clock the next morning, warning them to stay prepared, as this could change at any time.

My last night on the Tasman was certainly not going to be an easy one — now that *TTII* was slightly lighter she was being thrown around on the sea anchor like never before and my desire to get off the sea and onto land increased dramatically as the night went on. I wasn't the only one whose sleep was disturbed, though, as throughout the night Lisa's brother Riley would regularly wake Winton to continue plotting my course into the beach and make sure I hadn't suddenly changed my mind and decided to crash-land.

By 3 a.m. I'd had enough of the sea anchor and decided it was time to head to the beach, calling Lisa and letting her know I was going to start rowing. It was completely dark and rowing was incredibly hazardous. With waves partially rolling *TTII*, I had to be careful not to snap my last set of oars, and every couple of hours I would down a bowl of cold porridge and a few NoDoz to keep me going. I was waiting for the sun to come up and hoping to catch my first glimpse of New Zealand.

At this stage Lisa and Olly had rounded up the troops, sending numerous text messages to all the locals who were helping guide the landing party and all the supporters who wanted to come along. Winton was still plotting my course into Ninety Mile Beach and relaying this information to my surf-lifesaving friends, whose role it was to drive the inflatable rescue boats out to meet me.

A few more supporters had arrived through the night and by 5.30 a.m. Lisa and Olly had managed to coordinate a crowd of about 50 people outside the small school in Ahipara who were ready to make the 30 km drive up the beach to see me row in.

Olly announced they would all drive up the beach to a certain point before waiting to figure out the exact coordinates of my arrival. The convoy of 45 trucks headed up the beach one behind the other, trying to avoid waves that sometimes rolled in under their tyres.

Meanwhile I was rowing as hard as I possibly could, making some great progress. With about 20 km to go I stopped to watch the sun appear on the horizon and for the first time in 54 days I watched the sun rise from behind land. Seeing land kicked me into another gear and with adrenaline pumping I wasted no time getting back onto the oars and stuck into getting closer to the beach.

The convoy of trucks headed on up the beach with the odd one getting stuck and having to be hauled out by the others. Hovering above the convoy was a helicopter, flying out to visit me and fix my exact location for the landing crew.

My first visitor for the day would be the helicopter, followed by the boat a television crew had chartered to interview me while I was close to home. I immediately started to envy the two 200-horsepower engines on the back of this particular boat as I looked behind me to see the 15 km I still had to row. The TV crew hung around for close to an hour asking questions then had the nerve to start eating breakfast in front of me while I continued to row.

At the same time the Tasman gave me a parting gift and I was joined by another small pod of dolphins darting under *TTII* and surfing the swells with me. I was keeping in hourly contact with the land crew, who were now settled on the beach awaiting my arrival, letting them know my speed and current position.

Winton had positioned himself in the back of a truck, constantly plotting where I was going to land. Clouds had sent me a text me that morning, telling me this would be his last message and good luck for the landing. He also said there was going to be massive surf and to be very careful.

Concerned at the size of the surf, I called one of my surf mates, someone I could rely on to give an accurate estimate of exactly how big and powerful the breaking surf was. He told me the surf was very powerful with a number of sandbars and I should think very carefully about rowing into such large swells.

With only a few kilometres to go until I hit the beach I could see small dots all over the remote and slightly isolated spot and was surprised at how many people had ventured to the top of the North Island to see me land.

I decided to stop for some food and a small rest before starting the final push into the beach and I sat for some time about 5 km off the coast, reading through some of the notes I'd made about the safest way to land and the various safety aspects I needed to think about.

Rested and ready, I started to row again for the final time and I could now clearly see the outline of different trucks on the beach. To my sheer delight I was joined by a couple of guys on a jet ski, who had been following my progress. About 2 km out from the beach the helicopter flew out and hovered above me as my mates in the surf-lifesaving rescue boats drove out.

I set off a smoke flare so the guys could locate me and the moment I had been waiting for 54 long days was finally here. I was about to share an amazing moment with some of my best mates before deciding how I would get onto the beach. Olly joined the guys driving out to see me on his jet ski yelling out to me that it was the first time he'd ever seen my ribs! All the guys were laughing and teasing me about my massive weight loss. The inflatable boats nudged close and I decided to unload the important items from *TTII* before attempting to row her in through the 8 foot surf.

I passed over my computer and cameras and it was now time to think of a strategy to get through the huge breaking waves and onto the beach safely. By now we were floating about 600 m offshore and we knew we would have to act fast as I was almost in the break zone and the waves would be on top of us at any moment.

I desperately wanted to make sure *TTII* made it into the beach intact as well; she deserved it after keeping me alive for the last 54 days. I filled her compartments up with as much water as possible, significantly lowering her in the water. Hopefully, this would help her to right herself if she flipped in the rolling surf. Next I removed the rudder and gave it to one of the guys on a jet ski to drive into the beach rather than risk snapping it off over one of the four sand bars. The plan was to rig a small parachute off the back off *TTII* that would pull her straight as she was catching waves.

I removed my lifejacket and all the safety lines and started to row *TTII* into the beach. Large swells started to steepen behind me and I knew it wouldn't be long before one of them would pick us up. I saw a big wave building about 100 m behind me and started to pull on the oars a little harder to create some speed. The wave picked up the back of *TTII* and with just enough speed she started heading down the face. I had to move quickly, immediately throwing the oars overboard and jumping over the side with the parachute and rope. *TTII* sped down the wave as I sat there floating. I felt incredibly guilty for letting her crash through the waves alone, but knew it was my only choice.

TTII had gone ahead of me. I was floating out off the coast and like my father 34 years ago, I would have to swim to the beach and finish crossing the Tasman Sea. I had about 600 m to swim to shore and the surf was huge so it was clearly going to take some time to get in. With my lifeguard mates around me I started to swim, bodysurfing my first wave within moments. I was slightly concerned about whether I'd still be able to swim after 54 days on the boat, but this didn't seem to be a problem. And just like cleaning the hull in the middle of the Tasman, it was wonderful to be floating.

A helicopter hovered above me as I was swimming so that everyone on the beach could see where I was and as I got closer to shore hundreds of people moved towards me. I looked down the beach and saw that *TTII* had made it onto the sand and it was now OK for me to try to put my feet on the bottom and complete the crossing.

One of my lifeguard mates who had swum next to me all the way in stood up with his feet on the bottom. Without hesitating I did the same and felt the wonderful sand between my toes once again. I had done it. I had joined my father as the only other person to have rowed the Tasman solo.

As I started walking in to the beach I pulled out a New Zealand flag I'd stuffed down my pants and held it proudly above my head as crowds of people came towards me. I was greeted by Lisa, Mum and my brother Ben on the water's edge, as well as a number of reporters catching the moment I walked out.

With massive surges of water coming in I couldn't stay there for long and ran up the beach to a safer area for some more TV interviews. One of the radio stations had brought me a bacon and egg sandwich, which I immediately started eating and Winton passed me an energy drink.

I was absolutely amazed at the support I had received, with people travelling from all over New Zealand to see me land — one of my mates counted 90 trucks on the beach and over 300 people. Because of my agreement with TV3 I was unable to spend much time on the beach with other reporters, which also sadly meant I wasn't able to spend a lot of time with all the people who had come so far and made such an effort to support me. After all, driving along Ninety Mile Beach isn't like driving to a beach at the end of a road — you have to drive a long way along the beach itself and it's pretty remote country.

Within 10 minutes I found myself sitting in the back of a

truck with a bag of sultana bagels from my favourite bakery and about to drive down the beach. We were waiting for one of the reporters to find Lisa and when she jumped in we headed off — just me, Lisa and the TV3 crew, with me still feeling as if the entire moment was completely unreal.

Lisa had arranged a wonderful house for us to stay in at Ahipara, a small town about 40 km south of where I landed, and within half an hour we were there.

I sat and wondered what on earth I was meant to do now.

Epilogue

The night I arrived Ahipara was full of friends and sponsors. *TTII* had survived the beach landing with only a broken solar panel and I had lost a total of 21 kg on the expedition. I was paid a visit by two New Zealand Customs officials who quickly reminded me about the reality of life as they issued me with a warning notice, telling me I had broken a number of laws by not arriving at an official port of entry and not providing notice of arrival.

I found it incredible to hear them complaining about having no idea where I was landing, when 300 locals and supporters managed to get to the exact spot. The bureaucrats finally left and the house was full of my closest friends and family as we all sat down and watched ourselves on the news.

We stayed that night in Ahipara and headed back to Auckland for an intense week of interviews and media appearances. Lisa and I both struggled with this, as it added a significant amount of pressure to the time we got to spend with each other, but I knew it wouldn't be long until it was over and we could get back to normal life.

After 10 years of dreaming and two years of full-time work had led to 54 days of hellish rowing, I've been asked the same basic questions hundreds of times, all along the lines of 'Was it worth it?' or 'Why did you do it?'.

While I've tried to explain my trip in a number of different ways, I don't think there is a way to justify it to anybody. However, I think I did it for a number of different reasons.

Complete and absolutely selfish personal desire was a driving factor — I wanted to be the first person to row from Australia to New Zealand and experience the satisfaction of achieving that accolade for myself, my family and New Zealand.

Very early on in my planning I was sent two emails calling me an idiot and telling me I would most certainly die attempting the crossings. After I read them I decided never to respond to those people, as they sat there in their comfy armchairs, safe and boring at home. Instead I'd let my actions speak for me.

It wasn't so much that I made a decision to row the Tasman, but more that I felt I had some sort of entitlement and responsibility to do it and to complete the journey for our family. I realize now that personally I would have felt negligent if I'd never taken up the challenge and made the attempt.

I feel very strongly that I am incredibly lucky to have grown up in a country where adventure and the pursuit of extraordinary feats are encouraged and celebrated. Mountains were climbed, oceans were crossed and races were won through pure and utter Kiwi determination, ingenuity and courage.

I wanted to prove that New Zealand is still a breeding ground for success and adventure and I hope my children will grow up in a country where they will be less burdened by the tyre-kicking, nay-saying, tall-poppy-chopping personalities who tend to make themselves heard a bit too much for my liking in recent times.

The following phrase was scribbled onto the deck of both *Tasman Trespasser* and *Tasman Trespasser II,* and it accurately describes my feelings about why I wanted to cross the Tasman.

'Every man needs a little madness, or else he never dares cut the rope — and be free.'

The day humankind ceases to have the courage, the determination and the imagination to cut the rope and chase our dreams will be the saddest, most retrograde day of all for civilization, and I sincerely hope I'm not around when it occurs. We are all responsible for never allowing this to happen, by encouraging and supporting each other to find the rope by providing the blade to cut it.

Kia bloody kaha!

Appendices

i   Michael Buck, Land Manager

I remember Q telling me about five or six years ago that his main goal was to follow in his father's footsteps. Initially, I was blown away by his ambition and my reservations grew larger once I found out a bit more about his father's achievement.

My doubts increased somewhat over the next couple of years as his commitment to the ventures he undertook (uni, work, entrepreneurial stuff) wandered. However, when he committed, built a safety plan and created a Trust I knew he was in for the long haul.

Once boat construction began I knew he would attempt the crossing, no matter what. I was also confident in his safety plan and his research, but I must admit I was a bit concerned at his lack of physical preparation in the latter months, especially the minimal time he spent in the boat. What I never doubted was that Q was strong mentally, and ready for every possible scenario.

When it came to the failed million-metres, I thought Q looked incredibly strong over the first day, when he went a lot faster than his planned pace. In hindsight I wonder whether this is what possibly led to his body eventually breaking down.

It was quite remarkable to see him being able to switch off everything around him and focus on each stroke. While not being able to complete the challenge definitely raised a few questions about whether he could make the Tasman crossing, these questions were from others, not him. His ability to see the bright side of bad situations kept him sane and would be important for the lone Tasman crossing. My major concern was that if his body broke down and he suffered the same injury on the Tasman, he wouldn't be able to keep going.

Before Shaun left we'd decided that our phone calls would be about his position and that we'd keep them businesslike, so we could maintain some sort of focus. This meant that I didn't experience much of the downs, and I think this was left for Lisa to manage. I definitely felt his frustrations at the weather but at no time did he break down or question himself to me. It was wonderful talking to him when something great had happened and these were the calls I remember fondly — him telling me about the whale and the huge fin, and the albatross.

Even when the watermaker failed he stayed very calm and tried to stay focused and on track, and I knew Q was capable of achieving the crossing because it had consumed his life for years. Failure was never an option. I also knew he was mentally very strong and with his planning could tackle anything that arose. The only thing that I thought could stop him was if he ran out of oars. Shaun has always been mentally strong, with an ability to see positives, and he'd put together a well-planned campaign, built an incredible boat and had a solid support team of good people behind him.

On the negative side, though, I have to say he rushed a bit too much towards the end, he was so keen to start rowing, and looking back that watermaker had been an issue right at the start and we should have put more effort into getting it right, because if he hadn't been so close to New Zealand when it finally failed, he would have been in all sorts of trouble.

Planning his arrival was a huge issue. We initially believed Q had to come into Taranaki to make the whole venture worthwhile and his stubbornness about this was frustrating, but in the end there was nothing he could do. More than once we had almost confirmed orders for supporters hats and T-shirts only to have to cancel them at the last minute. In the end we realized we couldn't do anything other than be ready to plan the eventual landing within two days, so we turned our efforts into motivating Q to give it hell and actually make the country.

Missing his arrival was one of the hardest decisions I've had to make. Had it not been for the Taplin relay and my club mates, I'd have left Nationals early or not even gone. [A Taplin relay is a medley relay of four swimmers, four paddlers and four two-man dory teams.] We won the Taplin and the club did great, but it really didn't fill the hole of missing the landing and not being able to giving him a high five and a hug. For weeks afterwards I was gutted about it and concerned that Q felt let down. It was great to see others like Olly and Ash step up to help make it such a success, but to be honest I was a bit jealous as well. I'd done a lot of hard work and being there to welcome him would have been a neat reward and seeing others helping him ashore really sucked! I remember getting the call from Q letting me know he'd arrived. It was a massive relief and I felt a weight fall off my shoulders.

ii   Lisa Jones

Shaun first told me of his plan to row the Tasman after having a few beers on his 24th birthday. He said, 'If you're going to be my girlfriend, you'd better know that I'm going to row the Tasman.' What Shaun seemed to forget was that just the night before he had told me he was turning 24 on this birthday and not 27, as I had thought.

I wasn't sure we were going to make it through the next few weeks, let alone embark on something quite like rowing the Tasman. So when people ask me how I felt when he first told me, I usually laugh, as there were a few emotions at that time and the impact of him crossing the Tasman definitely hadn't sunk in.

Our relationship grew quickly and by Christmas, only four months later, I not only found I'd taken on a 24-year-old boyfriend who had just quit his job, but the true sense of the expedition he was about to undertake became apparent. Most young couples are still taking things easy at that stage, but suddenly a sense of almost dependence and support was developing and as Shaun's determination and enthusiasm for the adventure grew I quickly found myself fully involved in an expedition that was to take on a central part in our lives.

I never had any fear that Shaun wouldn't make it and maybe that was me being naive, but he was fantastic about including me in every step of the process right from the start. Knowing the risk-management plans and seeing how the campaign was coming together put me at ease.

When it came to the million-metre row friends and family around me at the time will tell you how this time was really hard for me. Shaun was facing a huge physical challenge and watching someone you love put themselves through something like that was never going to be easy. What was the hardest, though, was seeing Shaun lose his usual control and confidence. Suddenly, I saw him tired, barely being able to talk and saying things to me that made no sense. He'd done the row as a test of how his body would stand up to the demands of sleep deprivation and physical stress that would ultimately challenge him on the Tasman and while I was relieved that there was no sign of his epilepsy, the physical effects still worried me a bit.

I had my concerns that the time it took to organize sponsorship, build his boat and get the equipment and supplies over to Australia meant he hadn't put in the time he would have liked to do more training. What was great for me at this time was getting to know some of Shaun's friends better. Just seeing the support they showed for him through this event gave me strength knowing how many people were behind him and believed in him.

During the year leading up to Shaun's departure I was constantly inspired by his enthusiasm and determination. He often would come home and tell me of people who couldn't sponsor him, of money that hadn't come in and of various hurdles blocking his path, but I've never seen anyone continually see the positive side to nearly every situation as he did. This is what got him through a number of occasions where I think you and I would have seriously considered throwing it all in.

There were definitely times that were challenging for us as a couple. I would be lying if I didn't say that the new girlfriend being built and designed to Shaun's specifications and perfections made me slightly jealous. The endless weekends spent working on her, the endless time he would spend poring

243

over photos and design specifications trying to make her better would inevitably take time away from us just hanging out and going out with friends. The fact that Shaun wasn't working and had now moved in with me meant nights out came few and far between. Money was tight and time was precious. Then when the big date night to make up for all the time he was spending with this new bird was about to take place he cut his hand and it was another weekend in hospital.

Between having his appendix out and then the cut to his hand which left us spending hours in Middlemore Hospital, either sitting on the steps outside a ward waiting for surgery or being cooped up in a 4 m x 4 m waiting room with about 10 other people, we were spending quality time together — just not the quality we had in mind.

Getting over to Coffs Harbour made things become ever-increasingly real. Luckily, a good friend from university happened to be living there with her husband, who was a doctor, and as they were heading back to New Zealand we were able to stay in their house.

The first few nights we sat in a small hotel room realizing all the jobs we had to do — packing the boat, preparing food packs and sorting the final aspects of the trip. Looking back I can see how this would never have worked and with rapidly dwindling funds a house to stay in was a silver lining. A few weeks earlier we thought it was going to be just Shaun and me doing the final preparation and setting him off on his way. Despite all Shaun's positive energy and determination to get in that boat and set off, I think we both knew there was no way we could manage this alone. There was still so much to do and nothing took five minutes; it all seemed to take hours.

Our final days in Coffs would ideally have been spent relaxing on the beach, enjoying a few beers and organizing a big farewell party but this was not to be. My first day was spent in the boat yard with Shaun. There were about six other guys working on their boats in about 30 degree heat. Soon, I was attaching the steering cable and screwing the radar onto the boat, hardly something I'm qualified to do.

Michael and Olly flying over was a real lift for Shaun. Having his mates around was great and it was wonderful to be able to split the work among us and have a few laughs. My parents arriving the next day and Colin and Nitaya's surprise arrival from Darwin lifted our spirits further, and as we all set to work, the jobs started to get ticked off and the day of departure loomed closer and became ever more real.

Getting the final things packed up and down to the boat all seemed fairly surreal. Packing the boat took two hours instead of the 10 minutes we'd planned, but it was something we were getting used to and we both knew the final farewell was soon to come.

There was almost a sense of relief that morning — finally everything really had come together, Shaun had made it to the start line and his journey was about to begin. What was never going to be easy, though, was that final hug where I could see him and feel him and know he was safe but realize that this wouldn't be the case for the coming weeks. This was even more clear to me as he rowed out of the harbour and I was left waving him off on the wharf. Slowly, that little red boat which was to be his home for the next 54 days was lost in the swells.

Over the next few days it was interesting how dependent I think we both became on the phone calls. I knew he would be checking in with Michael every morning and evening and that I'd hear from him every few days but in those first few days, hearing his voice and knowing he was OK became the most important part of my day.

Over the next 54 days things in my life were supposed to be going on as normal and those who didn't know my situation (that my boyfriend was rowing alone out in the middle of the Tasman) would have thought everything was ticking along quite well. For the whole time my life went on hold and I never really gave anything 100 per cent. The old me, who would have gone into any situation giving my full attention, suddenly found myself attached to the phone, waiting to hear from Shaun and making sure that when he did call I was in a position to talk and give my full attention. This definitely didn't include being in a rowdy pub, not answering my phone for long periods of time or for that matter accompanying a friend on a speed-dating night for moral support.

I'm a physiotherapist, so during the day this was often difficult as patients are strolling through the door at regular intervals, expecting and deserving my full attention. Luckily, the day after the capsize I had a few cancellations just as Shaun called.

It was only then, when the danger was over and he was able to reflect on his situation, that the emotions came out. It's pretty hard listening to someone you love cry when they're so far away. It had finally sunk in for Shaun and for me how lucky he was not to have been hurt, and how lucky he was to still have all the oars and essential supplies so he could carry on. I knew he wished there was a concrete reason that would force him to call in a rescue and get him off that boat and home. However, we both knew he had to go on and he still had a few weeks at sea. When all you want to see is the finish line, to be told you are only two-thirds of the way is crushing.

The week building up to the arrival was pretty exciting. I couldn't wait to have him home and for this stressful time to be over. The difficult thing was trying to predict his landing.

On Thursday (four days before he landed) he rang me, concerned he was going to miss New Zealand. I laughed at first, considering I'd thought he was going to land on the west coast of the South Island the week before, I thought he was joking. This was definitely the wrong reaction. For him, as he sat out there alone, still hundreds of kilometres off the coast of New Zealand, missing the country was no laughing matter. His fear quickly became my own. I made a few calls to my brother and father, who met with me and talked through the options. Having Michael and Olly around was awesome as this was one burden I was happy to share.

I realized how serious it could be if he landed in the middle of the night, in darkness. We needed to be there, wherever he landed and I knew I was going to be there for him, ready to cater for whatever situation we found ourselves in.

The night before, all of Shaun's family were up there in Ahipara, with friends and support crew. Sitting around with the boys the night before and talking through how they were going to assist his landing started to calm me down. Having a great group of people around at a time like this I knew he wouldn't fail. There was a strong network there ready to help and support him through this final leg of the journey.

When I got the call at 3 a.m. from Shaun to tell me he was on the oars again there was a rush of emotion. I couldn't wait to get up and get going — he was finally coming home!

During the drive up the beach I experienced a mixture of emotions. At the start, in the early hours, I suddenly felt ill, perhaps I was excited but I was also pretty scared. This could easily turn nasty — there was a huge swell out there, it was dark, he was tired, he hadn't been eating properly for the last few days and the emotion of arriving was going to put him in a fairly vulnerable state.

When I could finally see him coming in the relief was huge. There were so many people there and the boys had headed out in the boats to meet him. I knew he was safe.

I would be lying, though, if I said it was all back to normal straight away. My boyfriend had suddenly become skinny, he had a beard, he walked funny and he never got off the phone to the media. Call me selfish but I just wanted him to myself — and so did everyone else.

This was his time to shine; his accomplishment was huge. I'd seen how hard he had worked over the last two years, struggling to cope with so many unexpected hurdles and he had finally overcome them all. It was his time to bask in the glory. Over the next few weeks I think we both found it really hard.

I was back doing some postgraduate study and had a block on at uni, hardly where I wanted to be when Shaun had just got back, but when I did stay home he spent his whole time on the phone and having meetings. My boyfriend didn't really get home until a few weeks later but at least he was safe, his mission accomplished and we could get on with a year that didn't include rowing an ocean.

iii   Colin Quincey

The message 'Hey Dad, I'm going to row the Tasman' to any other father would, I suggest, have prompted feelings of fear, stress, anxiety and lots of uncertainty about what it involved. For me this was not the case as, fortunately, I had 'been-there, done-that', having spent some four years instructing sea survival and another four assessing naval personnel for 'command' by pushing them to their mental and physical limits. I had a reasonable idea of what was involved. Or, in other words, in a practical sense, the 'uncertainty' factor and consequent stress was minimal. At the emotive level, on the one hand I was delighted that Shaun had decided to take up such a challenge; on the other I was never free of some anxiety. My initial response of 'That's a good idea!' (a hugely emotive and informative message!) did reflect my thoughts at the time. Fortunately for Shaun, my subsequent emails were more helpful.

For much of my life I've worked with young people and, from time to time, been somewhat disillusioned by their lack of initiative to 'challenge and to dare'. A consequence of the cotton-wool world we have created for them? To provide some motivation and inspiration to them was, in part, a reason for my own voyage, so it was therefore very pleasing to me that Shaun had decided to test the limits of his own human endeavour, and not at all surprising that I would offer 'unreserved support'.

The last paragraph of my book — the punch-line as it were — contains the words: 'Every man needs a little madness, or else he never dares cut the rope — and be free! The day that mankind ceases to have the courage, determination and imagination to do that will be very sad. We can only prevent that happening by allowing our young people access to the rope and giving them a knife if they want it.'

Shaun had already decided to cut the rope. He needed no motivation from me, but he got some anyway! When he asked me initially what my thoughts were about his trip, I told him I could totally understand how a trigger can spark off an idea — his was his own disappointing ocean swim, mine came when a trainee on *Spirit of Adventure*, when invited to climb the mast, said, 'Nah — what's in it for me?' My instant response was that there was something wrong here and what could I do about it? And just like Shaun, what I would eventually do about it had been under the surface for years.

A couple of key questions I asked him to think about early on was when had he last spent more than 24 hours without human contact, and why he chose a Tasman crossing when there were untold other adventures he could have. I also asked him if he thought he would have enough adrenaline and focus to carry him through all the boring crap, and enough mental strength and tenacity to make sound judgements when he was knackered, wet, screaming tired, cold and hungry? I asked my son if he'd ever faced those circumstances before, telling him that 'I don't know' was not a valid answer.

The last thing I wanted to do was divert or discourage him — I just needed to know he had thought through these sorts of issues. His responses were reassuring, and I told him that while I was still allowed to be cautious as a dad, 'Go for it' was my most important message to him.

One of the early conditions I laid down about any of my involvement was that it was to be 'Shaun Quincey's Adventure' *not* a 'son of Colin Quincey Adventure'. Though I could understand from a PR or sponsorship point of view that there was mileage in the family connection, it wasn't in my nature to get involved in that sort of thing.

In some areas his knowledge, contacts and experience were way superior to mine and I thought that his experience with surfboats was far more relevant than I had at the time I set out, so his CV was technically much better than mine, which would be significant when seeking sponsorship.

I knew I was also out of date with the technology. When Shaun told me he was going to be building his boat at Salthouse, I had a vague memory of some Salthouse kids watching my antics in the creek, and realized they were probably running the place by now. There would be some obvious PR benefits if they were able to help, and I reminded Shaun that while high-tech support was important, his critical kit would be his seat, oars, footbrace and rowlocks — these were hugely important for maximizing the efficiency of the 'human engine' his body would provide. It was critical that these were set up 100 per cent correctly and that they were also 100 per cent reliable. Rob H and others know all about how to do that.

His whole being, focus and reason for living once he was out on the Tasman would need to be to get out of there — and nothing, but nothing else matters! Rare moments to enjoy the whales or the birds or the sunset shouldn't be wasted, but, as I wrote in my book: 'Row, you bastard, row.' One good thought was that at least Shaun wouldn't have to worry about running out of smokes like his old man.

My advice to him about sponsorship was a suggestion to avoid any sort of deal that links 'getting there' with reward — for example, $2000 now and another $30,000 if you make it. This can lead to making bad decisions out there in a situation where, for example, you might be sick and you should be pressing the 'come and get me' button but that $30K beckons so you crack on and don't make it. It was vital that he controlled the project, not the sponsors. The opposite is a bad place to be and he didn't need that.

He certainly didn't need my advice about navigation — nowadays just press the 'where-am-I?' button and have spare batteries!

What I could help him with was the bit in the middle — when it would be all down to him. So we talked about sea anchors, ballast, safety gear and food: about 'rules', routines, self-discipline, decision making, sleep deprivation, sun, sore bum, etc., etc.

Despite numerous actual and potential setbacks I never doubted Shaun would get to the 'start line'. The determination, enthusiasm and energy necessary were always there. It was total commitment, as there has to be — anything less, as I well knew, wouldn't have been good enough. It was enormously satisfying watching him tackle the innumerable problems competently — he was much better at it than I ever was.

Having allowed the facts of the venture to sink into my mind it was time to reflect on the critical component of the venture — Shaun, the boat's 'engine'. The hardest part of the project would be the preparatory phase — getting to the start line, for which, aside from unconditional commitment, a whole range of managerial skills would be needed. I knew Shaun was good in this area — competent, efficient, organized and sufficiently 'pushy' to make things happen. So, in this respect, I would simply keep an eye on his progress and occasionally throw in some advice. On most occasions he already had it covered. A significant other area of concern would normally have been the practicalities and attitude to safety but with six years of surf-lifesaving experience Shaun was well equipped with this knowledge.

My reservation was his natural tendency to 'go for it', sacrificing thoroughness for expediency. 'Near enough is good enough' is fine for the vast majority of activities one undertakes and the consequences of not getting it quite right not generally harsh, but this was different. In this game the margins for error are minimal and the consequences can, quite literally, be deadly. So, we talked about this. Shaun was very much aware of this necessity; nevertheless, throughout the preparation and even during the voyage I regularly reminded him — at times, I'm sure, much to his annoyance.

The most important question in my mind was how Shaun would cope with being alone in a small boat in the unforgiving, unpredictable and very harsh environment of the Tasman but, of course, this was an unanswerable question, as it would be of anybody. You simply don't know until you've experienced it and, in the case of ocean rowing, there is really no way you can effectively create, train for or experience the scenario before-hand. It didn't actually help that I knew how I coped — Shaun is a different person. All I could do was ensure he gave it some thought.

Shaun and I talked through this stuff quite a bit. I felt it important that he should think about how he would react and thus, in a way, have some preparedness. Doing the 1000 km row was an excellent initiative, giving Shaun the opportunity to simulate the mental and physical stress he would experience.

When the human body reaches the limits of its endurance — mental and physical exhaustion, typically brought on by huge physical effort and/or sleep deprivation, it just wants to shut down. The faculties and senses function at very low levels.

253

Thought processes become vague: judgement and decision making are severely impaired. Alone, in the isolation of a small boat, this is a dangerous situation.

An effective way to combat these circumstances is to have a set of what I call 'the rules'. Many other adventurers have had similar routines. They need to be followed on a daily basis but become absolutely critical when exhaustion sets in. They must be very simple — they have to be because the brain isn't able to cope with anything more — but hugely important things that must be checked. They are there to ensure survival: safety harness on, doors locked, oars tied on, I must eat, I must keep warm, I must keep dry, I must sleep, etc., etc.

This is like a first line of defence. Self-discipline and willpower will be there in some measure as will a human being's phenomenal instinct for survival, but sometimes these states of mind need a bit of help.

It is very difficult to appreciate the importance of such very simple rules when you're sitting comfortably on the deck with a beer, so I hammered home their significance to Shaun many times. They were written on the boat's cabin wall so I guess the message got through. And, during the voyage, Shaun pretty much followed this sort of routine — with some notable exceptions.

During the voyage I made a point of not imposing on the management team. They were very well set up. Shaun had a job to do and shouldn't have time for unnecessary chat. I felt he only needed one point of contact to keep it simple and occasional social dialogue. I therefore directed any comments and advice to Michael, to pass on or not as he thought appropriate. This worked well. I spoke directly to Shaun about six times during the trip, while Michael did a terrific job throughout.

We made a surprise visit to Coffs Harbour a few days before Shaun left. My wife and I helped a bit with the boat — a canopy which proved to be useless, and packing food. I gave him some things to take with him, a couple of books — *Jonathan Livingston Seagull* was one; a picture of his grandma (my mum), which I had carried; a copy of Kipling's poem 'If' and a note on the lines of 'You've got a job to do — get on with it!'; some written prayers from Thailand; and, inevitably, a poster which said STICK TO THE RULES.

This was the first time I'd seen the boat other than a brief glimpse in Sydney. I was impressed but thought it needed more ballast. It was a terrific couple of days, and particularly good to meet up with most of the support team who were there.

I was spared the anxiety of knowing Shaun had capsized because by the time I got a call from Ben, he had righted and was sorting himself out with rescue authorities and his management team. I had lots of questions but thought it more important to let the team sort things out first. To me the priority question was what caused the capsize and how to prevent a recurrence.

The following day, in a long chat with Shaun, we were able to analyse the cause and come up with a solution which in fact was quite simple — trail a small drogue to counteract the impact of wind on the relatively high and buoyant stern when running down-sea. It wasn't until we were both back in Auckland clearing out the boat that we realized, through a chance remark, that the life raft had been a significant factor in the boat not righting quickly. It had fallen out of its stowage and hung underneath — effectively a weight holding the boat upside down.

It was evident from our conversation that this was a huge and scary trauma for Shaun. Though we never really discussed 'give up' or 'go on', he sensibly deferred the decision for a few days. I considered it took a whole lot of guts on his part to decide to continue and I felt very proud of him. I also thought it was the right decision. I'll never forget those words — 'I'm going to finish this.'

A big positive out of the incident was the lessons learned from the experience which could be applied to the rest of the trip. 'Stick to the rules' was one, another was controlling the boat down-sea — safety before speed.

I was concerned that media coverage had exaggerated the danger, and had not been accurate, etc. so after talking to Shaun, I sent the following 'informed opinion' note to family and friends.

… Although the www is very thorough and Michael's doing a terrific job with it, I thought I'd give you my take on Shaun's 'interesting' week and perhaps, thereby, some reassurance.

I keep in touch with Michael regularly, phone and email, to compare notes/thoughts/ideas and had a long talk to Shaun Wed night. We discussed the 'what happened and why' scenario of the capsize with the aim of ensuring it doesn't happen again. Basically Shaun was in uncontrolled drift mode — heading east so why not — in moderate seas. Seas and wind increased rapidly, the stern lifted above the crest of a sea and there, exposed to the wind, got blown 'ahead' of the bow causing the knock-down and subsequent capsize. Normally, the boat would have righted quickly but because Shaun was now lying on the roof of the cabin, that held the boat upside down until he shifted his weight. He kept his head and did all the right things at the time to restore stability. The solution to prevent recurrence is simple. Trailing a small drogue — enough to keep the boat lined up with the seas — will prevent the stern getting side-on and hold it down against a breaking sea or gusting wind. He can still make good progress but with a 'controlled' drift. Shaun will do this from here on. (TTI behaved differently in this situation — just sat side-on to the seas and bounced across the top, half rolling from time to time, shipping water — not particularly comfortable!)

Shaun had a hell of a fright and though admirably keeping his head at the time, some symptoms of shock followed — which is to be expected. We talked this through and Shaun was aware of them and how to deal with them. The biggest boost to morale is of course kilometres towards NZ which is happening and should continue for the next few days. The rain charts aren't looking good so the desalinator has to get fixed somehow. Once that's done, bit of a cruise into the coast and a Speight's in hand in say a couple of weeks! However, keep those fingers crossed and the prayers or whatever other device you may have to bring luck — he's still going to need that!

We can all be very proud of him. He's showing a lot of courage. He's having a rougher ride than I did.

I kept up communications with Michael throughout, and told him at one point that I thought it was very good that Shaun was taking time out doing some 'basics' — settling mind and body, as it were, after all the dramas and having some relative rest.

By this stage getting fully prepared for the final push was exactly the right thing to do, because I told Michael I knew he was now going to have to work for those kilometres, and that preparation for rain collection should be on his 'to do' list.

I also pointed out to Michael that Shaun's oars were now 'gold' and his single most important factor. He should fit a slack securing line to them 'just in case' and do no adventurous rowing that risks a break.

By then I felt his morale and confidence were probably OK again but I knew his thought processes and logical thinking were likely to have slowed, something that happens with accumulated stress. I knew Shaun needed to keep strictly to routines and stop-think before doing stuff to counter this. (Both Patrick and I had experience working with men who are under extreme mental and physical pressure and while Shaun wasn't anywhere near that state yet, and may never be, I wanted Michael to know that advice was available if it happened in future.)

When Michael asked for my thoughts on the landing I sent him the following list.

Some thoughts on landing:
- *The approach/tactics to landing site is the most important part of the voyage.*
- *The last 100 m is potentially the most dangerous.*
- *Landing through surf is OK as Shaun is extremely familiar with surf, BUT the boat is not a surfboat and if left uncontrolled it will roll. Suggest light drogue out over the bow, man oars to control direction and go with the flow, literally. Shaun mentioned he might break his rudder on landing — so what?*
- *SW gale on approach? He should consider sea anchor and wait for the worst to pass before landing. (Bloody hard call this and he probably won't!)*

- *Where? Needs beach of course and from Hokianga north there's lots of this but some nasty bits too. Rarely is the Hokianga Bar safe to cross in small boat. He could get very lucky but I would suggest extreme caution with this option. Ninety Mile Beach is an optimum target I would think. Vicinity of Ahipara perhaps ideal, certainly for logistics and, I believe, there are three hard-case pubs!*
- *Talk to the fishermen, they'll know better than anyone the hazards etc of landing locations.*

As regards the watermaker, it was never thoroughly proved before departure, despite mammoth efforts by the team and even though that brand has a very good track record I was always concerned about it. Would I have delayed departure to 'fix' it? No, but I would probably have taken more bottled water. It was a hard decision for Shaun; more weight means more effort to row which in turn means you need to drink more water. Sometimes you just can't win!

To have not had the water drop would have been stupid. You can't survive long dehydrated. I felt it was done very professionally — and good old Kiwi spirit to the fore — well done, John. I don't know what else was in the canister but a bottle of rum would have been good!

The armchair critics may say, 'Ah, but you weren't un-assisted' — to me this is pure bullshit and, in the overall context of the voyage, totally irrelevant. As far as assistance goes, Shaun had GPS, weather advice, 24/7 comms, none of which were available to me. Does this make his achievement less than mine — of course not!

In all manner of sporting competition technology moves on and records are broken because of 'assistance' from technology;

for example, the new streamlined full-body swimsuits, Kevlar sails on racing yachts, 'high-tech' rugby boots, aerodynamic and ultralight cycles — there are untold sporting advances going on all the time. What would such critics have us do — stand still so as to satisfy their petty obsessions with the rules? I am proud of my son, and what he did. No matter what else happens, we were the first.

No one can take that away from us.

iv Sponsors and supporters

Silver
Orcon Internet Ltd

Bronze
Timex Watches

Media partners
TV3 New Zealand
New Zealand Geographic
Radio Live Sport New Zealand
Rush Labs, Sydney, Australia

Charitable partner
Surf Life Saving New Zealand

Shipping and freight
Toll Logistics

Nutrition
Rebecca Yortt — dietician

Suppliers of equipment and services
Salthouse Boatbuilders
Eagle and Franich Construction — van
Bay of Plenty Helicopter Services
Cube Creative Print, Design & Signage
McMurdo New Zealand
Sea to Summit Outdoor Equipment
Back Country Food
Concept 2 Rowing New Zealand
Kiwi International Rowing Skiffs
Great Circle Life Raft Hire
Cross Fit Auckland
Harken NZ
Under Armour Clothing

Oakley Sunglasses
Horley's Nutrition
Kathmandu Clothing
Devonport Chiropractic Centre
Events Clothing Ltd
Wattie's Foods
RFD
BEP Marine
Healtheries Supplements
Rentokil
Coffs Harbour Marina
Coffs Harbour Boat Yard
Maxwell Marine
Coppins Sea Anchors
Voyager New Zealand Maritime Museum

Private donations and supporters

Catherine Allan; Tasha Harvey; Daniel Harvey and the
Harvey family; Riley, Rebecca, Jack and Maeve Lockett;
Nevil Pete; Kerry Trevet; Olly Young; Robert Voss; Fiona
Hastie; Rob Hastie; Deb Hastie; Cameron Pocock; Scott
Eagle; Mark Gribble; Richard Stevens; Julia McFadzien;
Beverly and Peter Brown; Nannette Quincey; Ben
Quincey; Megan Quincey; Joshua Fitzsimmons; Julia
Toomey; Elliot Mercer; Rebecca and Shae Borman;
Graeme Lee; Karen Lee; Michael Lee; Kate Lee; Rachel
Lee; Karen and Brian Cambell; Valerie and Grant
Morrison; Martin Fitzimmons; Richard Vaughan;
Matthew Bruce; Rebecca Yortt; James Brown; Andrew
Brown; the Lattey family; Gareth Pratt; Colin Quincey;
Matthew and Marilyn Moore; Chris and Ken Ingram;
Steven Gates; Tim Andersen; Winton and Jill Jones;
Grant Florence; Rod and Jenny Jones; Jess Berridge
Hart; Michael Buck; Matthew Coker; Tim Henricksen;
Michael Borlase; Laurie, Gwenyth, Karl, Michael and
Amber Margrain

V Equipment list and supplies

Personal clothing and effects

80 x daily food packs

58 litres of emergency water

1 x bottle of Glenfiddich Single Malt Whisky

1 x Musto Gore-Tex foul-weather jacket

1 x Musto Gore-Tex foul-weather pants

2 x quick-dry long-sleeve shirts

1 x Mairangi Bay Surf Club Speedos

2 x Under Armour compression pants

2 x Under Armour compression shorts

1 x polar-fleece vest

1 x polar-fleece hat

2 x sun hats

1 x pair of Oakley glasses

2 x books — *History of New Zealand* and *Jonathan Livingston Seagull*

1 x iPod

1 x polar-fleece blanket

1 x small micro-fibre towel

1 x thermal pants

1 x thermal long-sleeve top

1 x Timex Expedition watch

1 x Timex heart-rate monitor

Medical

2 x courses of general antibiotics

1 x tub of Sudocrem

2 x tubes of kill-everything antibiotic cream

2 x sunblock

4 x zinc sticks

130 x epilepsy pills

1 x small packet of sea-sickness pills

50 x codeine tablets

50 x Panadol tablets

50 x anti-inflammatory tablets

10 x antihistamine tablets

10 x constipation pills

10 x diarrhoea pills

130 x magnesium tablets

130 x multivitamin tablets

20 x NoDoz caffeine pills

1 x tub of aqueous cream

2 x blocks of antibacterial soap

1 x scissors

1 x self-stitching kit

2 x crepe bandages

1 x collection of plasters and dressings

1 x sling

Electrical system and equipment

1 x 150 amp-hour lead-gel battery

1 x Garmin GPS chart plotter

1 x WatchMate AIS Receiver

1 x solar panel

1 x HD digital camera

1 x Katadyn 40E watermaker

3 x 12 volt charge sockets

1 x fixed VHF radio

1 x Trac Plus Tracking System

1 x HP Compaq Presario laptop computer

3 x Sealite high-powered strobe lights

Emergency and safety equipment

    1 x Great Circle four-person life raft

    2 x McMurdo personal location emergency position
      indicating beacons

    1 x Trac Plus emergency location system

    1 x self-inflating lifejacket

    1 x satellite phone with spare battery

    5 x parachute flares

    5 x red flares

    5 x white flares

    1 x hand-held Garmin GPS unit

    1 x hand-held compass

    1 x small bottle of Jameson Irish Whiskey

    1 x hand-held VHF radio

    1 x cellphone

    1 x 5 days' emergency food rations

    1 x radar reflector

    1 x hand fishing line

    1 x mirror

    1 x fog horn

    5 x waterproof matches

    2 x manual bilge pumps

    1 x 24-hour online tracking system

Rowing and weather equipment

    4 x Concept 2 single-scull oars

    2 x Kiwi International Rowing seats and seat wheels

    1 x Coppins sea anchor

    1 x Coppins drogue

    1 x bulkhead-mounted compass

Daily food

- 2 x small bags of porridge mixed with nuts and dried fruit
- 1 x protein bar
- 1 x large Mars bar
- 2 x double-serve freeze-dried meals
- 1 x freeze-dried carbohydrates (rice or potato)
- 1 x multivitamin
- 1 x large bag of mixed nuts and chocolate
- 4 x Replace electrolyte drink
- 1 x bag of jelly sweets
- 2 x epilepsy pills

vi Boat equipment layout

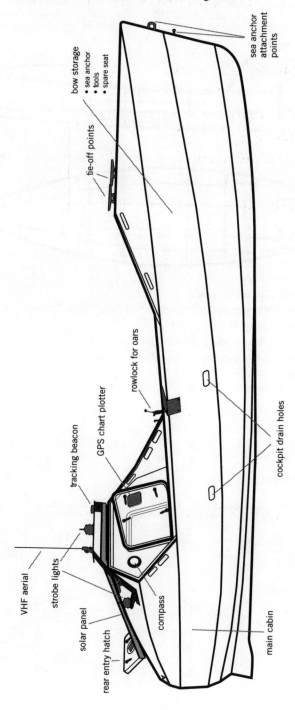

sea anchor attachment points

bow storage
• sea anchor
• tools
• spare seat

tie-off points

rowlock for oars

cockpit drain holes

tracking beacon

GPS chart plotter

VHF aerial

strobe lights

solar panel

rear entry hatch

compass

main cabin

vii Boat plans

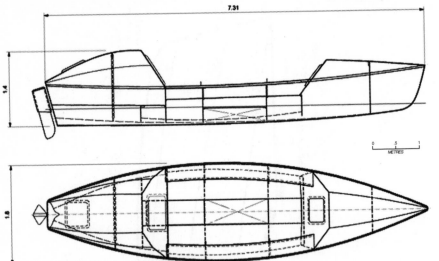

Tasman Trespasser II construction

Designed by: Phil Morison of Roswell and Adkin Boat Yards, England

Built by: Shaun Quincey and Dave Yallop

Built at: Salthouse Boatbuilders, Greenhithe, Auckland

Materials: Gaboon plywood, fibreglass and epoxy resin

Weight unloaded: 280 kg

Weight loaded: 650 kg

Paint: red Durapox paint

TASMAN TRESPASSER
GENERAL ARRANGEMENT

Colin Quincey

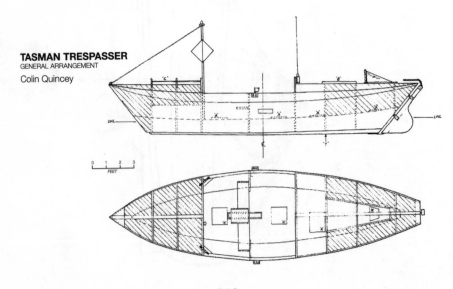

268

viii Parachute sea anchor

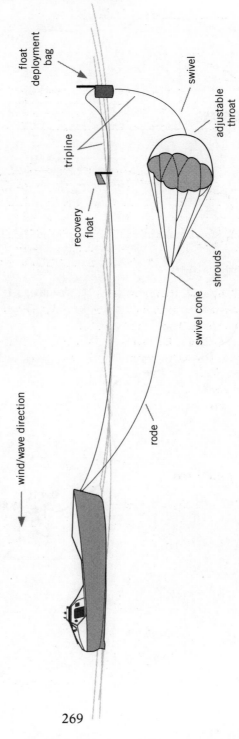

float
deployment
bag

tripline

recovery
float

wind/wave direction

rode

swivel cone

shrouds

swivel cone

swivel

adjustable
throat

shrouds

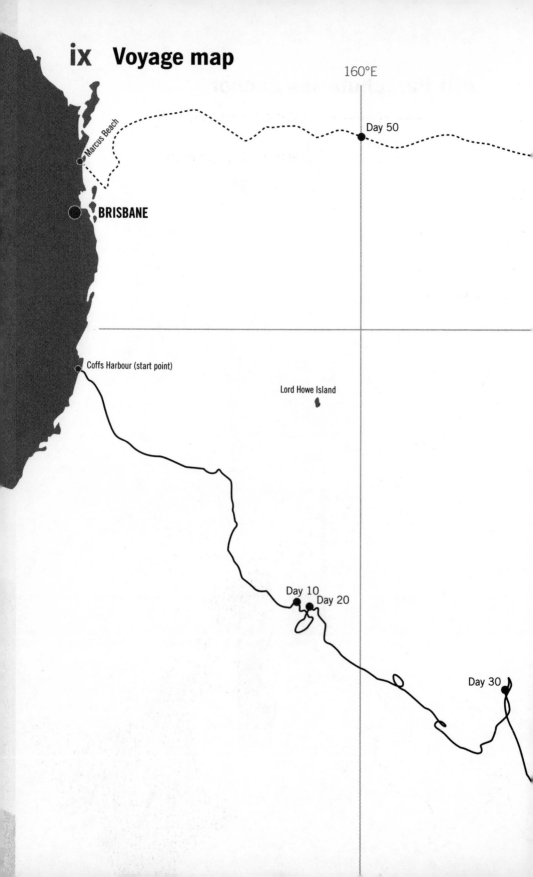

ix **Voyage map**

160°E

Marcus Beach

Day 50

BRISBANE

Coffs Harbour (start point)

Lord Howe Island

Day 10
Day 20

Day 30

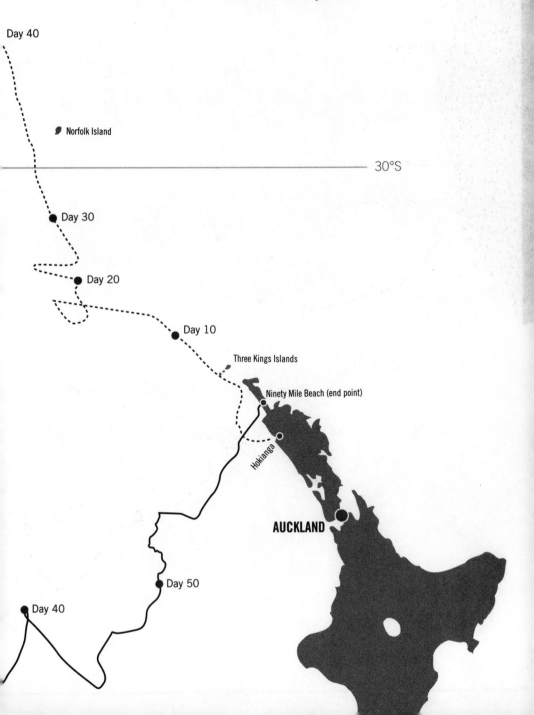